First
published
in 1933

FORCED LABOR IN THE
UNITED STATES

AMS PRESS
NEW YORK

FORCED LABOR
IN THE
UNITED STATES

by
WALTER WILSON

With an Introduction by
THEODORE DREISER

INTERNATIONAL PUBLISHERS

NEW YORK

14412

Reprinted from the edition of 1933, New York
First AMS EDITION published 1971
Manufactured in the United States of America

International Standard Book Number: 0-404-00239-0
Library of Congress Catalog Number: 76-144704

AMS PRESS INC.
NEW YORK, N.Y. 10003

CONTENTS

INTRODUCTION

It is a pleasure and a privilege to write an introduction to this book. Because of the outcry against the products of forced labor presumably being shipped into this country by Soviet Russia in order to undermine honest, well-paid American labor, Mr. Wilson set himself the task of establishing that forced labor is one of the outstanding characteristics of the American business world, and of its colonial extensions.

In his very interesting chapter, Forced Labor in the Colonies, Mr. Wilson devotes disturbing but also convincing space to the forced labor phases of the businesses of the United Fruit Company and the General Sugar Company in Cuba, the Firestone Rubber Company in Liberia, the Guggenheim tin mines in Bolivia, and other American companies having heavy investments in Central and South America, Haiti (The National City Bank), Hawaii (Sugar Planters Association), the Philippines. In this connection, he particularly emphasizes the section of the 1930 Tariff Act banning importation of goods produced by forced labor, which he points out was especially contrived to injure the Soviet Union.

As regards forced labor actually in existence within the United States, he dwells chiefly on convict labor, peonage and chain gangs, an awful—in the best meaning of that word—assemblage of horrors. He makes a point of the fact that our prison laborers are chiefly recruited from the ranks of poverty, and for small offenses, mostly petty thieveries due to poverty. The victims, through framed charges, forced confessions and the like, are finally landed in the ranks of the prison workers.

He seeks to establish that, outside our prisons, there are forms of contract and provisions of government and charitable relief which preclude free labor. And he adds the Marxian argument which makes it perfectly clear that, under capitalism, labor is bound, in any case, to be exploited, as it is.

I know that it will be argued that in comparing labor conditions in Russia and America he is presenting conditions not exactly parallel. It will probably be said that in America it is taken for granted that people must work, but that there is no legal compulsion. Whereas in Russia, they are compelled by law so to do, if they want to eat. And, while, frankly, there is involved here a fundamental difference between freedom and tyranny, the actual result is that there is tyranny here and not in Russia. That which will be ignored in this argument is the absolute proof that the fundamental business of the Soviet government, its philosophy as well as its official and technical structure, is devoted to the principle that it is truly of, by and for its people, and that all of the rewards of a properly functioning government must and do redound to the physical and mental welfare of all of its people. Whereas in America there have always been especial rewards and class privileges not for the really mentally gifted, but rather for the money-bag, the individual who centered on the business of accumulating money in its most tangible form, besides the direction and control of the government itself. For this would secure these properties and privileges for themselves and for their wives, children, relatives and friends to the third, fourth and seventeenth generations.

Mr. Wilson, throughout his carefully documented and verified study, lays very great stress on punishment, inhumane conditions and torture in the United States and its colonies, and there is no escaping the force of his argument any more than the volume of his data. It is overwhelming. In certain cases, it is of such nature as to be not only depressing but discouraging. And we're it not for the Marxian analysis of the inevitable process and failure of capitalism, it would be reason for complete social despair. But there is this philosophy, Marx' destructive analysis of the waste and the futilities of capitalism. And with this in the foreground, and taking into account whatever modifications so-called human nature in its race and state form may require, there is still the possibility of a more equitable and hence a better state than we have yet seen. I congratulate the author on his labors, and bespeak for the volume a wide reading.

Theodore Dreiser.

CHAPTER I

WHAT IS FORCED LABOR?

THE holy crusade of the past two or three years against "forced labor" in the Soviet Union has had one result certainly not desired by those who initiated the crusade. It aroused general interest in the problem of forced labor, which in turn led to the "discovery" that much forced labor exists in every capitalist country. In the United States, for example, where more discussion of forced labor has been generated than at any time since the Civil War, it has become evident that one need not go thousands of miles to Africa to witness forced labor in all its forms: there is enough first-hand material at home to satisfy the most thorough student of the problem. The old story: beams and motes, people in glass houses, boomerangs, and chickens coming home to roost.

Of course every one knows that there is some forced labor in the United States but how widespread is the practice is not generally recognized. This writer himself, who had done some work on the problem, never quite realized the extent until he made a special investigation during the past two years. Put a dot on the map of the United States wherever you find forced labor and you will find the fair face of this country covered with a close-mottled rash.

What is the meaning of the term "forced labor"? Generally speaking we understand it to mean work that is done by a worker in the absence of a "free" contract between himself and the employer. The United States Tariff Act of 1930 (section 307), prohibiting the importation of goods made by "forced labor"—including convict labor—and aimed at the Soviet Union, adopted the definition of forced labor given by the League of Nations. This definition, made by the Draft Convention of the Fourteenth International Conference of Labor at Geneva in 1930, states: "For the purpose of the present convention the term 'forced or obligatory' labor shall mean all work or service which is extracted from a person under the menace of any penalty, and for which the said person had not offered himself voluntarily."

By implication, this definition considers wage labor under capitalism to be voluntary or free and uncoerced by "the menace of any penalty." In reality, as we shall show, wage labor under capitalism differs from forced labor as the League of Nations defines it, not in content but only in form. Forced labor in the generally accepted meaning of the term—as applied to such types as convict labor, peonage, and chattel slavery—is a form of labor in which the "menace of a penalty" is more open and direct, in which all the elements of compulsion are unconcealed and evident to all.

Even when they enjoy personal freedom and outwardly, at any rate, enter into a "free" contract with employers, the labor of all workers in capitalist countries is forced labor. Karl Marx clearly shows why:

... Capital, in the social process of production corresponding to it, pumps a certain quantity of surplus labor out of the direct producer, or laborer. It extorts this surplus without returning an equivalent. This surplus labor always remains forced labor in essence, no matter how much it may seem to be the result of free labor.[1]

Under capitalism the employer hires the worker, that is, buys his labor power. But he hires the worker for the sole purpose of making as much profit out of him as possible. So, whether the fact is known or not, the worker actually toils a part of the time for himself and a part of the time without pay, producing surplus value and piling up profits, for his employer. Under chattel slavery the worker received food, shelter, clothes and medical attention. But no "free" contract on wages and other matters was made. Under serfdom the serf worked a certain number of days without pay for a lord and then was allowed to work the rest of the time for himself. Under capitalism the worker is made to believe that he enters into a contract freely. But when pay day comes he is given—in the aggregate—barely enough to buy food, clothes, and shelter which the slave or serf received for his work without worrying. Marx put it this way:

In point of fact, however, whether a man works three days of the week for himself on his own field and three days for nothing on the estate of his lord, or whether he works in the factory or workshop six hours daily for himself and six for his employer, comes to the same, although in the latter case the paid and unpaid portions of labor are inseparably mixed up with each other, and the nature of the whole transaction is completely masked by the *intervention of a contract* and the *pay* received at the end of the week. The gratuitous labor appears to be voluntarily given in the one instance and to be compulsory in the other. That makes all the difference.[2]

It is this surplus value produced by the workers and taken by the capitalists without giving any equivalent that is the main characteristic feature of all labor in capitalist countries. Working for another class, producing surplus value for the exploiters—this is the essence of forced labor.

But, it might be asked, where is the coercion in the production of surplus value? The worker is free, he is not kept under arrest, he is free to take any kind of work he pleases, or not to take any at all.

Under capitalism the worker is a proletarian, that is, he is deprived of the means of production and depends for a living solely upon his wages. He is without security for the future. He must take work from a capitalist to secure an income to exist. He is in no position to refuse to accept the employment offered him. He may escape working for a particular employer but he must work for some one somewhere in the system. Because he is propertyless, because he lacks the means of production he is *compelled* to sell his own labor power, to offer it for sale on the market like any other commodity. The penalty for refusal to work is death, death by starvation. "Freedom" to work, or not to work, narrows down to precisely that. It is the whiplash of hunger that serves as a most effective form of *coercion,* forcing the proletarian to work for another class.

The compulsion to work by hunger, created by the capitalist monopoly of the means of production and distribution, was recognized by the earliest of the capitalist economists. Karl Marx quotes one who said:

> Legal constraint (to labor) is attended with too much trouble and noise . . . whereas hunger is not only a peaceable, silent, unremitted pressure, but, as the most natural motive to industry and labor, it calls forth the most powerful exertions.[3]

Thus, under capitalism, there is no thought of abolishing forced labor, but merely of changing the *methods of coercion* to force workers to labor for another class. Instead of using direct force, depriving the workers of freedom, a more "peaceable, silent, unremitted" method of coercion is employed—hunger.

MAKING A "FREE" CONTRACT

Let us try to picture the way in which a wage worker in a company-owned American textile, coal or lumber town enters into one of these "free" contracts, implying an agreement between equals, made "without duress" and "with full understanding of all the obligations assumed." The steps taken by the "party of the first part," the capitalist, to prepare the minds and bodies of the "party of the second part," the workers, to sign this "free" contract are somewhat as follows.

A company in one of these towns shuts down its plant. Thousands of the workers suffer months of unemployment. The company threatens to import other workers at lower wages to take the jobs of those formerly employed. It prepares blacklists of those who may have criticized the company or attempted to organize a union. It cuts off credit at the company store. It may even evict workers from company-owned houses. Finally gun thugs, policemen and detectives attempt to terrorize the workers.

When the workers' ragged clothes hang limp on their starved bodies and when they have been terrorized sufficiently, the company, with the aid of its high-priced lawyers, draws up a contract. Usually the document consists of several pages of fine print which are full of "whereases" and conditions of every sort—all, of course, in the company's favor.

At last all is ready for the signature of the "free worker." Hundreds or perhaps thousands line up in front of the employment office in response to a notice that the plant is about to resume operations. All of them, according to capitalist theory, are waiting their turn to "bargain freely" with the corporation! Usually the procedure of hiring the whole line of workers takes only a few minutes. As soon as they sign their names or make their mark they pass inside the factory gates—hired after having exercised their right to make a "free" contract. And not a line or a word of the form contract, drawn up by the lawyers, has been changed!

In practice, the worker is often forced to trade in the company store, to accept as pay scrip which is redeemable only at the company store at a discount, and to live in a company house from which he can be evicted at the company's will. To incur the displeasure of the boss in one of these company towns means to be driven from the community.

The worker is bound to abide by the contract. In addition to hunger there are other penalties which prevent him from breaking it. Among them are the clubs of company thugs and policemen, the bayonets of the militia, poison gas, and the enslaving orders of the courts. An example of the latter is the injunction. The ultimate purpose of the injunction is to keep workers in a condition bordering on involuntary servitude, and its immediate purpose is to break the resistance of workers who try to bargain collectively. A great many cases of injunctions might be cited which have prevented union members and others from leaving, or threatening to leave, their employment without the consent of their employers.[4] And very closely related to the injunction is the yellow dog contract—a contract whereby workers "agree" not to join in any collective attempt to better wages or conditions no matter how bad these may be.

The most notorious yellow dog contract of the frankly anti-union type, and the form most widely used, is that which was employed by the Hitchman Coal & Coke Co. against the once militant organization, the United Mine Workers of America. It was upheld by the U. S. Supreme Court in 1917, and reads as follows:

I am employed by and work for the H. C. & C. Co. with the express understanding that I am not a member of the U.M.W.A. and will not become so while an employee of the H. Co.; that the H. Co. is run non-union and agrees with me that it will run non-union while I am in its employ. If at any time I am employed by the H. Co. I want to become connected with the U.M.W.A. or any affiliated organization, I agree to withdraw from the employment of said company, and agree that while I am in the employ of that company, I will not make any efforts amongst its employees to bring about the unionization of that mine against the company's wish. I have read the above or heard the same read.[5]

To give the appearance of mutual gain the contract hypocritically pretends that it is at the worker's special request that the company agrees to run non-union! Some anti-union contracts go further—the worker "agrees" in addition to have no dealings, communications, or interviews whatsoever with any agents or members of a labor union.

But on the other hand the "party of the first part," the employer, is not bound in any way. He has the privilege of interpreting the contract. He has the power to terminate it with or without notice and with or without reason. He can fire the workers in mass or individually. All that is necessary is to say, "Hey, there, you're fired!"

Thus the worker through his "inalienable" right of contract is whipped into signing himself into what amounts to forced labor just as surely as Negro slaves were whipped to their tasks in the South in pre-Civil War days. Friedrich Engels brilliantly summed up the whole illusion of freedom of the "free" contract when he wrote:

> The bourgeoisie have seized the monopoly of all the means of life in the broadest sense of the word; the proletarian can obtain the things he requires only from this bourgeoisie; they have the power of life or death over him; they offer him the means to live, but in exchange for a certain equivalent, his labor; they even allow him to harbor the illusion that he is acting on his own free will, without any constraint, like an adult person entering into a contract with them. But what a fine sort of freedom it is if the proletarian has no other choice but to accept the terms offered by the bourgeoisie or die of starvation, of cold, to live naked among the beasts of the forest.

The very existence of the capitalist state is proof of the existence of forced labor. The state is the organ of class domination, the organ of oppression of one class by another, "the national war engine of capital against labor." [6] It is the chief instrument of the capitalists in forcing the workers to submit to class exploitation. The simplest economic struggle, the smallest strike brings police to the factory gate to disperse meetings and arrest strikers.

The capitalist's life and death control over the "free" worker is shown most clearly in an economic crisis or at any other time when the capitalist chooses not to operate his factory. At such a time the worker finds the factory door shut in his face and no opportunity to do any work no matter how much he "volunteers." We have seen the methods of coercion used in forcing workers to toil. Now during the deep-going world economic crisis we see more clearly than ever the absolute power of the capitalist, who decides when the worker shall and when he shall not be employed. The worker is forced to acquiesce and lapses into involuntary idleness. Mass suffering, starvation and suicide follow. Marx pointed this out when he said:

> But capital not only *lives* upon labor. Like a master, at once distinguished and barbarous, it drags with it into its grave the corpses of its slaves, whole hecatombs of workers, who perish in the crises.[7]

CAPITALISM AS A MORE EFFICIENT SYSTEM OF EXPLOITATION

It has long been recognized that a worker in an industrial society does better and more efficient work when he is made to believe that he is working of his own free will. It is an accepted fact that the system of wage labor has proved to be more efficient in the exploitation of labor than outright slavery. Marx stated this fact tersely when he said:

> Capital has developed into a coercive relation, whereby the working class is constrained to do more work than is prescribed by the narrow round of its own vital needs. As a producer of diligence in others, as extractor of surplus value and exploiter of labor power, capitalism, in its energy, remorselessness and efficiency, has outscored all the earlier systems of production, those that were based upon forced labor.[8]

John Adams discerned the illusory character of freedom in wage labor under capitalism, as is shown in his speech in the American Continental Congress of 1777 when he said:

> It is of no consequence by what name you call the people, whether by that of freemen or slaves; in some countries the laboring poor are called freemen, in others they are called slaves; but the difference as to the state is imaginary only. What matters it whether a landlord employing ten laborers on his farm gives them annually as much money as will buy them the necessaries of life or gives them those necessities at short hand? . . . The condition of the laboring poor in most countries—that of the fishermen particularly of the Northern states—is as abject as that of slavery. [9]

Even southern slave owners, in defending their own system of chattel slavery during the slavery controversy in the United States in the 1850's, repeatedly pointed out the coercive character of "free labor" exploitation. Senator J. H. Hammond of South Carolina, for one, expressed this view in a speech in the United States Senate, March 20, 1858:

> The senator from New York said yesterday that the whole world had abolished slavery. Ay, the name, but not the thing . . . for the man who lives by daily labor, and scarcely lives at that and who has put his labor on the market, and takes the best he can get for it, in short your whole class of manual hireling laborers and "operatives," as you call them, are essentially slaves. The difference between us is, that our slaves are hired for life, and are well-compensated; there is no starvation, no begging, no want of employment among our people, and not too much employment either. Yours are hired by the day, not cared for, and scantily compensated. . . .

That such arguments by defenders of slavery were regarded very seriously is evidenced by the papers and pamphlets that were circulated by the defenders of wage labor trying to disprove the arguments.

The Maharaja of Nepal, having been "educated" by imperialism to recognize that wage labor can be more effectively exploited than slave labor, said in a speech in 1924:

> The slave must be fed and clothed whether he works ill or well, he must be nursed in illness, and at death or desertion his value will have to be written off as a loss. The slave will require more constant supervision than the free laborer, because, sure of a bellyful whether he works or not, he will naturally prefer to do the least possible; you cannot starve him, because his physical weakness will be your loss. The superiority of free labor to slave labor is not a matter of mere speculation. History has proved it and I doubt not that the experience of those who have occasion to use both descriptions of labor in this country will bear out the fact.[10]

Forms of Labor Under Imperialism

Capitalism resorts not only to indirect coercion in the case of wage labor but also to physical force when need arises.

Police, gangsters, prison, attacks on demonstrations, arrests of strikers and even murder are among the common weapons used to protect property and profits and to prevent the workers from effectively waging a fight to better their conditions.

But, in addition to this type of coercion, capitalism has need of other forms of forced labor. As one of its contradictions it also makes use of all the more direct types of forced labor, in which open physical and legal restraint is used. In every capitalist country direct forced labor is used, including, with variations, chattel slavery, serfdom, peonage, convict labor and imported contract labor.

Although both "free" wage and direct forced labor exist side by side in every capitalist country, it may be said that "free" wage labor predominates in advanced capitalist countries and direct forced labor in the colonial countries, especially the more backward. It is estimated that there are between 5,000,000 and 6,000,000 chattel slaves in the colonies to-day, chiefly in Africa and Asia.

The trend of labor under modern imperialism is toward a subtle transition from "free" to coerced labor in the highly industrialized countries. The emphasis during the nineteenth century was on freedom of contract and other "freedoms." But during the past few years these "freedoms" are being more and more openly curtailed as world capitalism finds itself in a permanent crisis. We see extreme examples of this under fascism in Italy and in the Balkans where all free associations of workers are prohibited, and the state drops its cloak of democracy entirely to reveal the naked dictatorship of the capitalists. In England a great many restrictions have been put on the right to strike, especially since the British general strike of 1926. In the United States the use of the injunction, the yellow dog contract, compulsory arbitration, and the police and courts place labor more and more under coercion, abrogating many of the civil and political rights which had been won by the working class during many years of struggle.

Paradoxical as it may seem, the trend in the colonies is just the opposite—from open and above-board forced labor to less open forms. There is a great deal of agitation at present against chattel slavery. This reflects, on the one hand, the fact that a different, more efficient type of labor is needed to man the new industries in the colonies. On the other hand, it reflects the struggle of the colonial masses against enslavement by the imperialists. Such "humanitarians" as those in the League of Nations and Secretary of State Stimson, in their recent outcries against chattel slavery, merely voice the need for a more concealed form of forced labor as a more efficient means of capitalist exploitation. They also hope their hypocritical protests will help to placate the rising tide of colonial revolt.

BORDERLINE TYPES OF FORCED LABOR

In the United States, as in every other industrialized country, the predominating form of labor is "free" or wage labor, which, however, exists side by side with much direct forced labor as defined by the United States Tariff Act of 1930. Other types of labor are also used, which are on the borderline between wage labor and direct forced labor. As we do not develop these borderline cases elsewhere in this book, a few words are necessary here to clarify the problem.

During the present world economic crisis of capitalism a great deal of semi-direct forced labor has developed in connection with unemployment relief. No study of the volume or effect of this type of forced labor has yet been made in the United States although we know that it reaches enormous proportions. Scarcely a day passes but that the press reports such cases.

This unemployment "relief" forced labor is of two general kinds—work for a private or government agency, and work for a private employer who secures his labor through some government agency.

Work for agencies or institutions may range from the time-honored wood-cutting of the Salvation Army to road building for the state or Federal government. Usually eight hours or more of hard labor are required in return for enough food for just bare subsistence and a bed in a "flop" house, or, if the worker has a family, for enough coarse food to maintain life and a shack or dingy room to sleep in. Under a plan used in California three thousand men were recently forced to build a thousand miles of motor roads and mountain trails for the state. An American Legion official in Michigan has proposed a plan for that state which he says is modeled on that of California, under which labor camps would be established where workers would do road work without wages. But they would be given food worth 22 cents and a shelter worth three cents for a day's work.

Perhaps most of this type of forced labor for a private employer is to be found in connection with unemployment "relief" through the so-called public works programs. Municipalities and states allocate sums from public funds for the construction of roads, bridges, canals, etc., "to provide work for the unemployed." The contracts are given to private contractors, who offer the unemployed a chance to work at wages from 40 to 60% lower than the usual rates for similar work. Those who refuse to go to work under such conditions are removed from the register, deprived of further relief, and even in extreme instances, arrested or threatened with arrest for vagrancy. Workers have also had their names removed from the list of registered as a penalty for their activity in the unemployed councils. In some cities unemployed who refuse to work for flop house fare are "deported" from the city limits in droves.

One of the most recent and typical reports of forced labor in the form of unemployment "relief" is from Bakersfield, California. Labor groups there, according to a *Federated*

Press report, June 3, 1932, had protested that employers, including well-to-do farmers, were using the relief agencies as employment offices. "The welfare bureau," says the report, "because it has the power to bestow relief where and how it desires, can force men to work even though the wage is not sufficient to buy food for the family.... What is it but forced labor to tell a man with wife and children that he must work for 15 cents an hour if he wishes the county to aid him?"

Similar reports on "work relief" have come from over a hundred communities including Philadelphia, Chicago, Milwaukee (Socialist-controlled), Cleveland, Baltimore, Kansas City, Pittsburgh, Houston, Hartford, Indianapolis, Louisville, Buffalo, Toledo and Trenton. Still other reports reveal the same conditions in agricultural sections, especially in the South during the cotton-picking season.

And one of the chief offending agencies is the Red Cross, which during the 1930 drought gave out a dole of $1.55 a month per person to the neediest cases in the stricken sections of the South. U. S. Senator Burton K. Wheeler charged that the organization was forcing laborers to accept work for private employers at 15 cents an hour. It was also charged that the Red Cross made the workers pay off private debts by this kind of enforced labor before relief was given.

Such use of forced labor is not new in the history of capitalism. Marx, in describing the cotton crisis of 1861-1865, said:

The cotton employees willingly offered themselves for all public labors, drainage, road-building, stone breaking, street paving, which they did in order to get their keep from the authorities (although this amounted practically to an assistance for the manufacturers). The whole bourgeoisie stood guard over the laborers. If the worst of a dog's wages were offered, and the laborer refused to accept them, then the Assistance Committee struck him from their list. It was in a way a golden age for the manufacturers, for the laborers had either to starve or work at any price profitable for the bourgeois. The Assistance Committees acted as watch-dogs.[11]

Less recognized but very important sources of forced labor in the United States are orphan homes, religious homes for children, government schools for Indian children, poorhouses, insane asylums, and similar institutions. Some of them are veritable slave-driving institutions. Unfortunately, no study has ever been made of them but it is commonly recognized that they all exploit direct forced labor, in fact, hard labor imposed on inmates of these institutions is an American tradition. An example of the sort of thing we mean is indicated by an admission from Mrs. Franklin D. Roosevelt, who is connected with the Rome School for mental defectives, that girls from that institution were being exploited in private homes for 60 cents a day, the "wages" being paid, not to the girls, but to the state.[12]

We are more fortunate in having definite documentary evidence of the lot of some 38,000 American Indian children, wards of the government, between the ages of six and 18 years, who are forcibly taken from their reservation homes and parents at the age of six and put in government boarding schools several hundred miles away. There they are made to perform all sorts of forced labor under conditions of unbelievable horror—often for private profit. In the summer many of them are forced to work in the beet fields of Kansas and Colorado as child laborers where they are often beaten and confined for not doing their work "properly." Many of them contract tuberculosis and trachoma in these government institutions.[18]

Another type of forced labor in the United States is that performed in connection with floods and other disasters during which both private and public employers conscript workers to build and repair levees and do other emergency work. The least little freshet in the Mississippi River or any of its southern tributaries serves as an excuse for conscription of Negro and white workers. The writer personally remembers workers who were afraid to go to the vicinity of Hickman, Kentucky, during a flood for fear of being conscripted, and their danger is even greater in such states as Louisiana, Mississippi, Arkansas, and Alabama. Forced labor similar to levee building is found in connection with fighting forest fires in the West.

The difference between the various systems of exploitation of labor is not that forced labor exists under one system and not under another. The difference lies in the method of coercion used for extracting surplus labor from the workers. For the purposes of this study, we may accept the definition of forced labor as used in the Tariff Act, keeping in mind, however, that this definition covers only *direct* forced labor, and by implication considers wage labor under capitalism to be really free. In our concluding chapters we will have occasion to point out under what conditions free labor can exist when we analyze the charges about "forced labor" in the Soviet Union and contrast the form of labor there with that under capitalism. The main purpose in this book is to consider the forms of direct forced labor in the United States and in the colonies directly or indirectly under its domination.

CHAPTER II

CONVICT LABOR

WHO ARE IN PRISON TO-DAY?

UNDER capitalism forced labor, in one form or another, is recruited from free labor, so that both forms of labor are to be found side by side. As the world-wide economic crisis, which began in 1929, deepens and leaves its indelible and fatal marks on American capitalism, causing decay in all phases of economic and social life, retrogression to the older and more direct form of forced labor becomes more and more accentuated.

To meet the economic crisis American capitalism has forced the working masses to bear the brunt of the burden in the form of unprecedented unemployment, one wage-cut after another, the split up of available jobs among a larger number of workers with corresponding reduction in average earnings. This impoverishment of the working class has caused a great increase in the prison population. Individual workers, on the one hand, have been forced to commit "crimes against property" in order to remain alive. Other workers have been thrown into prison on political charges for participating in struggles growing out of the workers' battle against starvation.

Prison labor forms one of the largest and most constant sections of forced labor, and it has always been recruited almost entirely from the working class and poor farmers. Most of the inmates of prisons are not "criminals" at all but victims of capitalism. A great many are young workers.*

* Police Commissioner Edward P. Mulrooney, of New York, in a speech reported in the New York *Times*, May 9, 1932, said: "The majority of our criminals to-day are only boys. The records of the

24

There have been a few frank admissions, even by capitalist spokesmen, of the truth of this class analysis of the prison population. None of the admissions is more outspoken than an editorial in the Raleigh, N. C., *News and Observer,* December 27, 1930. Said the editorial:

Look at the chain gangs, jails and other penal institutions in the country and state, and we arrive at one of two conclusions. Either education and wealth are two of the strongest fortifications against the commission of crime, or there is a different measure of justice for the rich and the poor, white and black, intelligent and ignorant.

Almost without exception, the inmates of our great institutions of correction are from the lower classes, seldom having more than a grammar school education. Moreover, they are found to be of the poorer classes. A good many are black, which is easily explicable in view of the fact that there are few rich, and few educated, Negroes in the South.

Many other such admissions from the ranks of the "educated and rich" could be cited. For example, Colonel Edward B. Stone, principal keeper of the New Jersey State Prison, declared the recent unprecedented flow of prisoners into New Jersey institutions was caused by unemployment. Over half of the persons convicted were imprisoned for stealing. Warden Lewis E. Lawes in his *Twenty Thousand Years in Sing Sing* says that most of the younger prisoners at Sing Sing were convicted of robbery: all of the 16-year-old prisoners, 91.7% of the 17-year-olds, 70% of the 18-year-olds, 81% of the 19-year-olds. One can easily see the implications of such statements. Who are the unemployed? Who are likely to have to steal to live?

Austin H. MacCormick, assistant director of the United States Bureau of Prisons, recently stated that out of about 120,000 prisoners investigated over 70,000 "have never received organized training for an occupation, and about that number are unskilled workers. Nearly 40,000 have voca-

New York City department show that almost 70 per cent of the persons arrested for felonies in the last year were young men between the ages of 17 and 20."

tional training that is inadequate in terms of their intelligence rating." [1]　In other words this authority says that at least 110,000 of a prison population of 120,000 are unskilled or poorly trained workers.　This estimate is very conservative. MacCormick in a still more recent address stated that 60% of all American prisoners have not gone beyond the sixth grade; 25% are virtually illiterate, and 10% completely illiterate.　To interpret these facts, ask the question: who is likely to be illiterate in the United States?

Bennet Mead, statistician of the Federal Bureau of Prisons, has found that property crimes showed a big increase from 1910 to 1927.　The economic crisis has caused a further great increase in petty property crimes.　For example, officials of the New York City Department of Correction have admitted that the city's 18 penal institutions are overcrowded with almost 6,000 inmates, though their total capacity is about 5,300.[2]　This record has not been approached since 1914.　Officials of the Department were forced to admit that a large part of the increase resulted from petty crimes which could be traced more or less directly to poverty and unemployment.　Some prisoners, they added, committed small crimes deliberately to obtain food and shelter for several months.

The New York *World-Telegram,* August 28, 1931, carried a survey by George Daws, staff writer, which said: "Three of every four men who go to Sing Sing Prison from New York City pass through the big gates because of crimes involving money. . . . And the money for which these men risked—and lost—their liberty averaged only $30 for each crime."　And an editorial in the same paper commented:

No wonder the Wickersham Commission threw up its hands and refused to make a report on the causes of crime.　Most "crimes" are crimes against property.　The causes are chiefly economic.　To state those causes is to indict our mis-named Christian civilization and to expose the barbarity and the inefficiency of our dog-eat-dog economic system.

Poverty, slums, unemployment, and social injustice are the crimes of our system against the individual—yet we call our victims "criminals." Prohibition laws and other such unenforceable laws are merely secondary and passing breeders of lawlessness.

The Wickersham Commission had aroused even this capitalist paper's ire by reporting, "We find it impossible comprehensively to discuss the causes of crime." The Commission did not explain why it found it impossible. Certainly not because of lack of facts.

BIG CROOKS GO FREE

Under capitalism the petty crooks and racketeers give a "cut" out of their spoils to the really big crooks—politicians, capitalists and government officials. When a racketeer is sentenced, which is very rare, it is usually not for criminal activities but for ot paying his tribute to the government and its officials. Witness Al Capone and scores of others, including American Federation of Labor "business agent" racketeers, who have collided with the "law" for falsifying income tax reports. Take as an example of the "business agent" racketeer type, Theodore M. Brandle, New Jersey (A. F. of L.) labor "leader." On April 4, 1932, he pleaded guilty to defrauding the government in income tax reports. He and his partner, Joseph F. Hurley, a former state Assemblyman, were forced to pay to government and court officials $88,721.65 of their loot in taxes, interest and fines.

A cabinet member like Albert B. Fall, former Secretary of the Interior, steals and receives bribes of $100,000 and over. He is sentenced to only one year's imprisonment. In prison he is treated like a distinguished visitor. After serving nine months and 19 days he is released. A part of his sentence was a fine of $100,000 and he was to remain in jail until the fine was paid. But the authorities waived a small matter like a $100,000 fine and permitted him to go free. The fine stands as a judgment to be paid when, and if, he gets the money, which observers say is doubtful. He was not even required to take the customary pauper's oath. Harry Sinclair, oil magnate, also went to prison for a short rest for stealing Teapot Dome oil lands. He was given practically all the comforts and services expected in a first-class hotel.

Wholesale bribery in federal prisons, by which wealthy convicts have won transfers from Atlanta and Leavenworth to the comparative comforts of army detention camps, was recently exposed. Among those transferred in this way were George Graham Rice, convicted in the sale of $3,500,000 worth of valueless securities; Larry Goldhurst, financial adviser to Bishop James Cannon, Jr., in his Wall Street gamblings—Cannon went free; and John Locke, sentenced to three years after the $8,000,000 failure of the brokerage house of Cameron, Michael & Co.[8]

It is, of course, only in the most exceptional case that a rich man goes to jail, even to be showered with such attentions and courtesies. The cases of imprisonment of wealthy persons are so rare that when one occurs the capitalist newspapers almost invariably contend that democracy has been vindicated. "There is one justice for the rich and poor," they chorus.

But what about workers? A starving worker steals a ham for his family as did Oscar Josey, a Negro of DeKalb County, Ga., in 1930. He got 20 years at hard labor on the chain gang. Caspar Wright of Asheville, N. C., steals a pound of butter and gets a long "gang" sentence. John Creek, an Annapolis, Md., Negro, steals a chicken and gets five years in the pen for it. In North Carolina in 1931 a Negro was sentenced to death and then given a commutation to life imprisonment for stealing a pair of shoes.

It often happens that a court gives a small fine to a worker for a petty property law violation. Court costs are added to the fine and the worker goes to jail for a long term to work off both the fine and court costs. In one case in Alabama a young boy was fined $1 but got court costs assessed against him of $75. There are thousands of American Jean Val Jeans who steal for starving families and get long forced labor sentences.

What Are the "Crimes"?

What are some of the common crimes that fill the prisons with victimized workers? They include petty property crimes, liquor law violations, vagrancy, union organizing, violation of injunction, strike and other labor activities. Besides these there are the various frame-up charges. Scores of examples of the use of the frame-up against class war prisoners could be cited.[4] Among the best known are those of Sacco and Vanzetti, Mooney and Billings and the Scottsboro boys. Working class girls have been framed up by the vice squad of New York and other cities.*

"Sedition" and "criminal syndicalism" are other crimes fastened by the ruling class on rebellious workers in railroading them to the penitentiary. An example of a "sedition" charge was the case, in a Pennsylvania steel town, of Peter Muselin, Milan Resetar and Tom Zima, workers who were sentenced to five years' imprisonment and $500 fine each for the "crime" of possessing and reading Communist literature. In October, 1931, Resetar died of tuberculosis contracted while in the Allegheny County Workhouse—a notorious forced labor prison—after all efforts to obtain adequate medical treatment for him had failed.

A good illustration of the use of a "criminal syndicalism" law to fill the jails with workers is shown in the coal strike in Harlan County, Kentucky, in 1932. Every striker or sympathizer was considered guilty of this "crime" and scores were arrested and thrown into jail with this as the only charge.

* Judge Samuel Seabury in his report on the investigation of the New York Magistrates' Courts, in referring to the vice squad, third degree, etc., was forced to admit that "The abuses that have been disclosed do not strike at people of wealth and power. They oppress those who are poor and helpless. . . ."—New York *Times,* April 3, 1932.

But one may ask: "What about justice? The worker has recourse in the courts, hasn't he? He has the right to trial by a jury of his peers? How is injustice possible under such conditions?" Liberals still have illusions about "justice" and "equality" under democracy and under capitalist laws, but workers are beginning to understand that there are two kinds of "justice" in this country—one for the poor and one for the rich. The courts are stacked against the workers. For every witness that the worker brings forward, the state and the prosecutors can hire a dozen perjurers, as they have done repeatedly in frame-up cases against militant workers. Other practices like denial of counsel, mistreatment of witnesses, improper jury lists—especially no Negroes on juries in the South—and scores of other abuses, the Wickersham Commission found to be "habitual and routine practices." One hundred and fifty cases were reported to this commission where trial came so soon after arrest that no time was permitted for defense.

Third Degree

But one of the chief methods by which workers are forced into prison labor is through their own "confessions." These "confessions" are secured by torture—by the third degree. As the Wickersham Commission was forced to admit in its report on law enforcement, third degree tortures are reserved especially for the unemployed, the unskilled, the foreign-born, the Negro, and militant union workers.

The courts, the prosecuting attorneys, the capitalist newspapers, and the police would have us believe that the torturing of helpless prisoners in the jails of this country are isolated events, a "perversion" of police powers. Such is the purpose of all the "investigations." Particularly horrible third degree methods come to light and immediately the "investigators" get busy. They find evidence which eliminates certain policemen and police officials from their jobs. But the effect of such investigations is to cover up the fact that the third degree is an established institution and a useful weapon under a capitalist system.

The third degree is applied with special ferocity to Negro workers, both in the North and the South. Consider the recent case of Yuel Lee (Orphan Jones) who was tortured by Maryland police for 16 hours without sleep. A club was broken over his head; he was tied and a light flashed in his eyes. When he was too exhausted to know what he was doing, he was made to sign a paper which he did not read. The police claimed that this was Lee's "confession."

Another example of this refined democratic court procedure against workers was the shooting in a Birmingham jail of Willie Peterson, framed-up Negro worker and ex-soldier, by a white lawyer, Dent Williams, while the prisoner was being subjected to the third degree by the sheriff, police and Williams.

In Arkansas, two years ago, it was found that the Sheriff of Helena, as well as a long line of sheriffs before him, had used an electric chair as a part of the third degree, care being taken not to give enough "juice" actually to cause death.

The Wickersham Commission reported the case of a Negro boy in Arkansas who was whipped for six consecutive days. It found that in Texas Negroes charged with crime or arrested on suspicion were flogged with heavy leather whips on bare buttocks. This whitewash "investigation" commission found many specific cases of third degree torture. A woman was taken from a sick bed to the Denver police station and kept awake, starved and grilled from 2 A.M. Sunday until Thursday night under unspeakably filthy conditions. A prisoner in Miami, Florida, was chained to a floor in a room infested with mosquitoes. New York prisoners were beaten by police with baseball bats. Of 166 recorded cases of the third degree in New York City in 1931, more than half were for first offenders and 67 were boys between 15 and 20.

No torture is too severe or bestial for the guardians of "law and order" to use to obtain "confessions" from workers. Police choke suspects, pour water through their noses, beat them with rubber hose, strike men's sex organs, keep prisoners awake for days, terrorize them, handcuff them upside down, spray them with tear gas, and not infrequently murder them.

The worst third degrees and prison tortures generally are reserved for the political prisoners. Political prisoners are working class fighters and organizers who are thrown into prison because of their convictions and activities in the labor movement. In prison they are given the hardest and most disagreeable work to do. They are punished severely for minor infractions of rules. They are deprived of privileges and kept under constant surveillance and suffer many other special disabilities.

The harsh treatment given politicals in the Allegheny County Workhouse at Blawnox, Pennsylvania, is typical of treatment given such prisoners all over the country. There have been 22 mine strikers incarcerated in this workhouse. A newspaperman who visited there recently wrote:

In the workhouse there are many men sentenced to as high as five years, particularly in the case of class-conscious workers. Ordinarily persons sentenced to two to five years are sent to the Western Penitentiary in Pittsburgh. However, this is considered too easy punishment for striking miners and they are sent to the workhouse where conditions are much harder and the food much worse.

Thus it is clear that victimized members of the working class furnish the prison forced labor. They are secured by the operation of discriminatory laws, by frame-up, by the third degree and other practices resulting from conditions inherent in capitalist society. This important class fact has been largely overlooked or covered up not only by capitalists but by liberals, prison reformers, and even by the official labor movement as represented by the top-leadership of the

American Federation of Labor. All these groups have shed maudlin tears about protecting the "public" from convict-made goods but about protecting the unskilled worker or about the welfare of the convict slaves little has been said and nothing done.

CHAPTER III

EXPLOITING CONVICT LABOR

OF all the many kinds of forced labor in the United States, one of the most important is the use of convicts. Its extent can be partially grasped by looking at some official and unofficial estimates of the total annual value of merchandise made in the prison factories, mills, shops, and farms of the United States.

When one attempts to secure such figures one finds that very few official studies have been made, and none of them recently. The figures issued by the United States Bureau of Labor Statistics in 1923 are still the most comprehensive ever brought together.* According to these estimates, the total value of commodities produced in 104 state and federal civilian prisons for adults in 1923 was $75,622,983. The value of goods placed on the market amounted to $44,843,355. Goods consumed in state or governmental institutions and public works accounted for the rest. The above commodities were produced by 51,799 convicts out of a total prison population at that time in the 104 prisons of 84,761. This estimate does not include juvenile reformatories, city or county prisons, federal military prisons, or the maintenance work—prison upkeep, cleaning, laundry, repairs, cooking and so on—done in every prison. About 25,000 convicts were used for maintenance in 1923.

The state with the greatest value of prison goods produced in 1923 was Alabama with close to $7,500,000.** Next came

* The United States Bureau of Foreign and Domestic Commerce attempted in 1926 to bring some of the 1923 figures up to date, but the 1923 study by the Bureau of Labor Statistics is still recognized as containing the most authentic and comprehensive data.
** Road work is included in these estimates.

Kentucky with over $7,000,000. Georgia was third with over $5,000,000. Other leading prison-labor states, each producing over $2,000,000 worth of goods in 1923, follow in the order of their importance: Michigan, Maryland, West Virginia, Minnesota, Wisconsin, Connecticut, Tennessee and Oklahoma.

The latest estimates conservatively give the population of the same type of prisons studied in 1923 as 140,000 on January 1, 1932.* It is estimated that at least 70,000 of these are productively employed, as against slightly over 51,000 in 1923. Almost 35,000 of the 1931 prisoners were employed at maintenance and the remainder were either not reported or were reported incapacitated or idle.

Because of the greatly increased number of prisoners employed, and because of the improvements in machinery and methods of employment, prison production of goods in 1930 was undoubtedly considerably greater than in 1923. But because commodity prices and rates paid to the state for the use of convicts have dropped so sharply since the beginning of the economic crisis the dollar value of the goods may not be very much greater. However, if a recent unofficial estimate is anywhere near correct, then both the volume and value of goods were much greater in 1930 than in 1923. This estimate, made by the Associated General Contractors of America at their San Francisco convention in 1931, gave 75,000 as the number of employed convicts in 1930, producing goods with a market value of $100,000,000. Additional weight is given this estimate by a statement two years ago by Senator Harry B. Hawes of Missouri that $40,000,000 to $50,000,000 worth of convict-made merchandise moves in interstate commerce annually.

* *American Year Book*, 1931, p. 535. Note the gain in prison population. There were 7.5% more prison commitments in 1931 than in 1930. Prisons are now about 70% overcrowded.

Convict Labor in State Prisons

Minnesota does an anuual business in prison-made farm machinery and binder twine of around $3,000,000. The twine output amounts to over 20,000,000 pounds annually, along with 3,000 rakes, 3,000 mowers and the same number of binders. These goods, incidentally, are sold principally in Minnesota, North and South Dakota, Wisconsin, Iowa, Nebraska and Montana.

Alabama has one completely integrated prison textile industry. Cotton which is grown on the prison farm is ginned, dyed, woven into cloth and made into shirts in Kilby Prison.

The warden of the state prison at Michigan City, Indiana, reports that 1,806,804 shirts, 71,875 pieces of furniture, 23,572 pairs of shoes, 8,800 rugs, in addition to many other commodities, were produced in that prison in 1928.

Warden Lawes of Sing Sing Prison in New York recently admitted that the fiscal year 1931-32 has been the most prosperous the Sing Sing factories have ever known. For the first nine months, beginning with July, 1931, sales totaled $860,000, as against total sales of $800,000 the previous year.[1] Auburn Prison also produces annually about $1,000,-000 worth of goods consumed by state departments.[2]

Massachusetts, according to the Boston *Evening American*, which recently ran a series of articles on prison industry in that state, does an annual prison-goods business of over $1,000,000. Kentucky in a single year produced 1,102,295 shoes, in addition to large amounts of other goods, of which 95% was sold outside the state.

San Quentin prison in California, where Tom Mooney and other political prisoners are held, made 3,996,947 jute bags during the fiscal year ended June 30, 1927. The return to the state was $399,644. Mooney himself every day of the year sits in a small unventilated washroom and peels potatoes for 700 meals a day.

A report of an investigating committee from the Tennessee

legislature in 1931 said: "In this time of depression this prison (Nashville State Penitentiary) has not only been self-sustaining but it has actually been paying a profit into the state treasury which last year was over $100,000." Profits for this prison in 1927-28 amounted to $266,697.

FARM, ROAD AND CONSTRUCTION WORK

The big prison-farm states, Texas, Arkansas, Louisiana, and Mississippi, work their convicts largely in agriculture. Nearly 250,000 acres of land in the United States are under cultivation by convicts. Texas alone has 83,407 acres farmed by prisoners, raising products which were valued in 1927 at $1,362,958. Louisiana in 1926 had an income from her prison system of $1,557,715. This income from the forced labor of prisoners obviously helps to keep down the tax rates on the big plantations in these states and is hence heartily approved by the capitalists and big landowners.

Professor N. B. Bond of the University of Mississippi, in reply to a recent questionnaire sent him by the writer, said: "Many thousand bales of cotton are grown each year by convicts. Sale is made to the highest bidder. The cotton is shipped anywhere the buyer wishes." In a four-year period ending June, 1928, Mississippi prison farms paid $2,354,260 to the state, while stocks accumulated and cash on hand amounted to $375,687.

In 1923 work done by convicts on roads and other public jobs was valued at over $15,000,000 for the entire country. In 1927 prisoners in Virginia alone, according to Warden R. M. Youell of the State Penitentiary at Richmond, did $4,000,000 worth of road work.

There is also a great deal of construction work done by convicts for government institutions. Out of 98 institutions listed in the *Handbook of American Prisons and Reformatories* for 1929, 35 were using convicts on construction work. The largest of these undertakings are the $7,200,000 prison at Attica, N. Y., the new Eastern Penitentiary at Gratersford,

Pa., the new Illinois State Penitentiary, the new Michigan State Prison at Jackson, the State Prison Colony in Norfolk, Massachusetts, and others, including the $3,000,000 job on the U. S. Industrial Reformatory at Chillicothe, Ohio.

LOCAL AND COUNTY CONVICT WORK

Much less is known about the convict work in city and county lockups, workhouses and gangs. Dr. Hastings H. Hart, prison authority, reports that there are 10,860 such city and village prisons in towns with 500 population and up. In addition there are about 3,000 county prisons. According to Dr. Hart, 1,600,000 prisoners were committed to these prisons from January to June, 1930.

The jobs done by prisoners in these jails in all parts of the country range from the crudest common labor, such as crushing rock, to highly skilled typographical work. They include road and bridge work, construction of buildings, and manufacturing, especially furniture and clothing.

In the South, in particular, city and county prisoners are exploited to the utmost on roads and farms as well as in other prison industries. Florida, Georgia, North Carolina, South Carolina, and Tennessee have a large number of prisoners convicted of misdemeanors—usually law violations carrying a sentence of less than one year's imprisonment—doing road work under county management. In Georgia 69% of all those convicted of misdemeanors are so employed. Louisiana, Arkansas, and Texas have farm work largely for this type of prisoner.

Outside the South we find such cities as Toledo, Columbus, and Dayton, Ohio, working their prisoners on farms. In Massachusetts eight of the local jails and houses of correction work their convicts in chair, shoe, and shirt making. Most misdemeanants in New Hampshire do farm work. Connecticut has 10 county jails doing work ranging from chair making to laundry work for women.

In Pennsylvania eight counties employ prisoners at road

work and other public jobs, such as bridge building and construction. Nine counties employ prisoners at farm work. The Philadelphia County Prison has 2,906 prisoners at various kinds of work. The Allegheny County Workhouse, which serves Pittsburgh and where a number of political prisoners are now incarcerated, has a broom factory, a carpet factory, a chair factory, laundry, upholstering shop, and farm.

Although there has never been any estimate of the total value of work done and goods produced by convict-slaves in these city and county institutions, it must amount to tens of millions of dollars.

SYSTEMS OF EMPLOYING PRISONERS

This great volume of convict-made goods, valued at around $100,000,000 for state and federal institutions alone, and at many millions in addition for city and county institutions, is produced under several different systems. The most important systems are the "contract," the "state account," "state use," "public works," and "lease." There are a few others, either combinations of the above or schemes devised to get around state laws regulating the marketing of convict-made goods.

The "contract" system is one of the oldest and most disreputable of all the convict labor systems. As early as 1867 prison contractors were flourishing in all except three prisons in the country. Under this system a private business man or firm contracts with the state for the use of a certain number of convicts. The private contractor then sets up machinery in the prison, provides raw material and sets his convict-slaves to manufacturing some commodity. The state feeds, shelters, guards and otherwise takes care of the prisoners for the contractor, who sells the products made by the convicts in the open market wherever he can. In 1923, prisons in 19 states used some form of contract, and goods valued at around $30,000,000 were produced for contractors and sold. There has been very little, if any, change in the use of this system since 1923.

Then there is the "state account" system under which the state goes into business on its own, manufactures or produces goods and sells them on the open market in competition with other goods made by "free" labor. Oftentimes the states set up dummy companies to market the goods for them.

Under the "state use" system convict-made goods are not sold in the open market but consumed in the state's institutions. In 1923 only 11 states used this system exclusively and there has been little change since.

Under the "public works" system convicts are used in construction or repair work on public jobs, such as roads, public buildings, and the like.

The "lease" system has perhaps the longest and most sordid record of all. Under it a convict is rented or hired out entirely in the custody of a private business man or company. The prisoner virtually belongs to the contractor, who has complete authority to guard, feed, discipline and exploit him as he sees fit. The modern lease grew out of the Civil War. Prior to that time convicts in the South were white workers and farmers. But after the "freeing" of the slaves the prison population rapidly became black workers and peasants. Negroes convicted of minor "crimes" were hired out to private business men under slavery conditions. It was undoubtedly a deliberate move by the ruling class to secure forced labor on a large scale as a partial substitute for chattel slavery.

The best citizens and biggest companies made fortunes in the traffic and exploitation of leased convict-slaves. Confederate generals, colonels, senators and justices of the supreme court were among the big dealers. General Joseph E. Brown, ex-chief justice of Georgia, and his son, Julius, the late General Joseph M. Brown, and General John B. Gordon, ex-United States Senator, are Georgia's outstanding examples of convict-slave leasers. The Tennessee Coal, Iron and Railroad

Company, now a subsidiary of the United States Steel Corporation, was one of the biggest companies to be founded on convict labor. This company, as well as others, dealt in convict labor "futures" in the same way that gamblers deal in wheat and corn "futures."

It is no overstatement to say that the conditions inevitable under the lease system have been more horrible than under any other penal system in the modern world. In spite of the fact that the lease is "illegal" in several states it is still used to some extent and is legal for certain types of convicts in North Carolina, South Carolina, Arkansas, Louisiana, Florida, and Kentucky. Florida legislated against the lease system—for almost all of its prisoners—in 1923, following the whipping to death on a chain gang of a young North Dakota boy, Martin Tabert. Alabama abolished the lease in 1928, following the exposure of the death of a young white convict named Knox, who was deliberately scalded to death in a laundry vat at the Flat Top mine operated by the Sloss-Sheffield Steel Co. Prior to the scalding he had been brutally whipped with a steel wire the thickness of a man's finger. After his death the warden who witnessed his death had bichloride of mercury pumped into the body to simulate suicide. He was murdered because he could not perform the amount of work required.

PRISON-MADE COMMODITIES

The wide range of prison-made goods includes almost everything imaginable from baby buggies to coffins, from lumber to flags, and from farm machinery to cotton. Work clothing is the most important. In 1923 production in this one field was valued at around $18,000,000. According to one of the foremost authorities on the subject, A. F. Allison, of the International Association of Garment Manufacturers, the competition in the work-clothing line has grown steadily since 1923. The National Federation of Women's Clubs estimated in 1926 that 41% of all work shirts and 35% of all work pants were convict-made. A single prison contracting firm in 1923 produced in its 17 prison factories about 16,000,000 shirts.

Next in importance among prison-made commodities is twine and rope valued at $5,543,000 in 1923. Of all binder twine made in the United States, 21% is prison-made. The value of work done by prisoners on farms amounted to $5,200,000. Close after farming came shoemaking valued at $5,363,000.* Prison-made furniture was valued at $2,970,-000. Then came brooms and brushes, $1,604,000; hosiery and underwear, $1,565,000. Lumber, which was valued at $728,000, is further down the list but is mentioned here because of its special interest in relation to the cry of Soviet "dumping" of allegedly convict-cut timber. In addition to the above, road construction, repair, and general work on public jobs were valued at over $15,000,000.

Several hundred commodities are made in prisons. Probably the most extensive list of them was that sent to the 70th Congress, First Session, by a group of about 75 prison wardens. But even this list was by no means complete. The wardens' statement reads:

In the southern states cotton, grain, sugar cane and livestock are produced by convict labor; in others turpentine and lumber; in others granite, marble and agricultural limestone is quarried; in Missouri and other central states sheep, hogs and cattle are raised and slaughtered on penal farms and the surplus sold. In Oregon flax is raised on farms and processed by convict labor. In many other states fruit and vegetables are canned on penal farms and gardens; in the great wheat-growing states of Minnesota, Wisconsin, Kansas, Indiana, Oklahoma, Missouri and the two Dakotas binder twine and farm implements are manufactured by convict labor and sold to the farmers in those states; in other states scrub brushes, rat traps, rag rugs and rag carpets are made; in others work shirts, work clothing, overalls, shoes, brooms and mops; in a few states coal is mined from state-owned coal mines by convict labor. In some states

* Coal was mined in 1923 which was valued at over $4,000,000, but declined in 1928 when Alabama took its convicts out of the mines.

juvenile offenders, male and female, are employed making knit goods, embroidery, baskets, books and a variety of other wares.

The wardens might have mentioned also many other kinds of convict work, especially roads, bridge, and general construction work, as well as the huge new industry manufacturing license tags for automobiles.

"Manufacturers" of Prison Goods

A large part of the convict-made merchandise is made under contract for and distributed by many concerns, some of them well known. The following list gives only a few companies among the many engaged in this business:

Salant and Salant Mfg. Co., Inc. (shirts), New York City, which has contracts in several prisons, including Florida, Tennessee and Iowa; the Reliance Mfg. Co. (shirts) of Chicago, with several subsidiary companies; the Worthy Mfg. Co. of Chicago, with contracts in Connecticut, Indiana and Kentucky prisons. Then there is Oppenheim & Co. of New York City, which contracts for a part of Delaware's prison labor. The Kentucky Whip and Collar Co. of Eddyville, the Hoge Montgomery Shoe Co. of Frankfort, and the Meyer Bridges Co. of Louisville have contracts in Kentucky prisons. The Jones Hollow-Ware Co. of Baltimore contracts for labor in Maryland, Gray and Dudley Hardware Co. of Nashville in Tennessee, the Parker Boot and Shoe Co. in Missouri. The Dearborn Furniture Mfg. Co. of Chicago contracts in Iowa. The Schoonmaker Chair Co. of Concord uses a part of New Hampshire's prisoners, the Ascutney Co. (shoes) of Windsor, a part of Vermont's. There are many other companies in many different lines.[3]

Marketing Convict-Made Goods

Many ingenious and effective devices have been developed for getting rid of the enormous quantities of goods produced in the prisons of the United States. For instance, states which are not allowed by law to hire out their convicts directly have established the "piece price" system, which the Wickersham Commission called an "attempt to circumvent restrictions of the contract system." The Commission called it more iniquitous than the infamous contract system. Under this system a state buys raw material from a contractor and works it into manufactured articles which it then sells back to the same contractor. Other states have been known to establish dummy companies to handle their convict-made goods, selling them with their prison-made character concealed.

Prisoners are commonly forced to sew what they know to be false labels on garments and other goods. It is a matter of record that prisons of various states have supplied large mail-order houses, chain stores and department stores with great volumes of prison-made shoes, stoves, brooms, furniture, house-dresses, overalls and aprons which have been sold under false labels. Thus the prisoners are being "reformed" by being forced to put false labels on goods they have made.

In 1927 practices of this sort came to the attention of the Federal Trade Commission and it was forced to investigate. One case reported was that of the Commonwealth Manufacturing Co. of Chicago. This company's only facilities for "manufacturing" were a 15 by 20 foot office and a single desk. Yet it advertised far and wide the prison-made shoes, clothing and binder twine that it claimed to have "manufactured."

The Commission reported that the shoes sold by this company "contained branded on the soles thereof the letters 'U. S.' . . . surrounded by the shield of the United States, below which appeared the brand 'Munson Army Last,' with the full knowledge and consent of the warden of the Indiana State Prison."

The most cunning of all tricks, however, is that of using popular and "patriotic" labels. Masquerading under this guise an enormous volume of goods move in the markets of nearly every state. What "patriot" wouldn't buy Gray and Dudley's "George Washington Stoves," or the "Liberty Stove," both of which are made in the Nashville penitentiary? Similar convict-made brands of work clothes are the "Uncle Sam," the "American Eagle," the "Big Yank," the "Army," and—as a special appeal to southerners—"Dixie Dan." If one can be so disloyal as not to fall for an appeal to flag and country there is the "Gridiron" or "Big Nine" for sportsmen. But for solid comfort get the "Roomy Richard." All of these are prison-made shirts. And on the 4th of July one can buy a flag and help the prison industries! In 1925 a single women's reformatory in Massachusetts made 4,368 state and national flags.

Incidentally, convict labor was used for other "patriotic" purposes in 1930-1931 in the following instances: clearing underbrush from Kings Mountain in North Carolina in preparation for Hoover's prosperity speech there in 1930; work on streets in historic old Arlington, Virginia, home of the "unknown soldier"; and work on the Arlington Memorial Bridge across the Potomac leading to the Lincoln Memorial in Washington, D. C. Prisoners were also used on the Lee Memorial Boulevard in Virginia.

Not only are prison-made goods sold in the home markets. *They are also dumped abroad in huge quantities.* It has been unofficially estimated that 10% of all convict-made merchandise is exported. Members of the House of Representatives from the big prison-farm states declare that of the hundreds of thousands of bales of cotton produced by prisoners, about 65% is exported. The cotton is not labeled and is sold in the general market.

In 1927 Canada stopped the importation of convict-made goods from the United States. The action followed the indignant protests of Dominion manufacturers at the dumping of prison-made hosiery and work garments into Canada by prison-labor contractors on this side of the border.

COMPETITION WITH "FREE LABOR"

Arthur Brisbane, the popular bourgeois columnist, has recently been quoted as saying that "We don't let our convict labor compete with free labor; and ought not to allow Russian convict labor to compete." The second part of this statement relating to the Soviet Union we will deal with in Chapter IX. But as for the first, Mr. Brisbane obviously has not read the official bulletin, *Prison Industries,* made public by the United States Bureau of Foreign and Domestic Commerce in 1929. Speaking of convict-made goods it said:

The effect of placing on the open market a volume of goods which has been produced below normal costs is to lower prices and demoralize the market. While at any time this practice tends to bring about unfair competitive price conditions, the effect is more keenly felt when there is over-production. The increase in prison production which is predicted, will make it difficult if not impossible for manufacturers employing free labor to continue operation in trades where the prison output becomes heavy. . . . The fact that the volume of displacement of some prison-made products is small, does not mean that the effect on the market is negligible. But it may be, and often is, a serious factor in demoralizing price levels.

Mr. Howard B. Gill, superintendent of the State Prison Colony, Norfolk, Massachusetts, recently said:

The reports [of the U. S. Bureau of Labor Statistics.—*W. W.*] for 1905 and 1923 devote considerable space to the effect on free industry of competition of convict-made goods, setting forth an array of evidence which leaves no doubt that prison industries, by underselling, by dumping, by false labeling, by unfair advertising, by unscientific accounting, by brutal treatment of labor, and by bad management, have been able to take advantage of free industry to the detriment of both labor and capital. The evidence presented is not confined to any one system of production, distribution or management. It persists under the State-Use, the Public Account, and the Public Works and Ways systems—all government-controlled, as well as under the Contract, the Lease, and the Piece-Price systems which are under private control.[4]

The fact that all systems of convict-merchandise production offer competition to "free labor" is not generally recognized. The fact is, of course, that the state use system, which is popularly supposed to furnish no such competition, in reality does offer the same competition as any other system. It is obvious that if the prison industries did not make auto license plates, school desks, and other goods, then "free labor" would get the job of making them.

As pointed out in *Prison Industries*, "Certain of the major factors in the normal cost of production which must be met by all manufacturers are entirely absent in the case of prison industries." These frequently include rent, taxes, light and power, and labor costs, which are always lower. For the use of its convicts the state usually receives from the contractor from one-sixth to one-third of "free labor" costs.

Julian Leavitt, a well-known student of the prison labor problem, in a series of articles in the *American Magazine* some years ago described a contract in the New Haven (Conn.) County Jail. He reported that "For the sum of 8 cents a day the New England Chair Company, alias the Ford-Johnson Co., has been getting the labor of an able-bodied man together with food, clothing and shelter for the man; together with a factory building in which the man might work; together with heat, light and power and armed guards and keepers to see that the man works."

Kate Richards O'Hare, after a prison-labor survey in 1925, told of a contract that the Oklahoma State Prison at McAlester made with a large work clothing contractor. It provided that the prison should establish a plant for the manufacture of work shirts and women's house-dresses; that the state should provide a suitable shop and storage rooms, heated, lighted and ventilated; furnish the necessary electric power to operate the plant; furnish cutting tables, benches and other necessary fixtures, keep the inmates fed, clothed, housed and under good discipline, enforce the "task" set by the contractors, and transport all raw and finished materials.

Some idea of the effect of dumping convict-made goods on the market is shown in the case of an inland state which during the early part of 1925 sold over a million dollars' worth of work clothes for what they would bring. The market was demoralized for more than a year and a half.

Another effect of cut-throat prison-labor competition on "free labor" was brought out at the convention of the Associated General Contractors of America in 1931. In the states of Virginia, Florida and Alabama wages of free labor are beaten down to 10 and 15 cents an hour by prison-labor contractors seeking contracts in competition with other contractors. Due to prison competition in South Carolina contractors are now able to hire "free" unskilled labor for as little as 75 cents a day.

In Oklahoma Governor "Alfalfa Bill" Murray, during 1931, was selling prison-made ice at 20 cents a hundred pounds cheaper than ice made by "free labor." He has threatened also to enlarge the prison bakery and sell prison bread in all parts of the state.

Another example of the direct effect of such competition was shown by Peter J. Salmon, official of the American Foundation for the Blind, in hearings before Congress in 1928. Mr. Salmon testified that "there has been set up a competition with which neither the blind nor any other free labor can compete. . . . Prison-made brooms are sold so cheaply in the open market that they constitute a menace to the large number of blind-made brooms, the principal industry for the blind." Other fields where the blind are meeting serious prison-labor competition are in making rugs, brushes, mops and chairs.

Convicts have even been used a number of times as strike-breakers. One of the first examples was in the Coal Creek strike in Tennessee in 1891-92. When the forces of the state had overpowered the miners, after an intensely bitter war, an official of the Tennessee Coal, Iron and Railroad Co., in an interview with the New York *Times,* said: "One of the chief reasons which first induced the company to take up the system [convict-lease] was the great chance it offered for overcoming strikes. For some years after we began the lease system we found that we were right in calculating that the free miners would be loath to enter upon strikes, when they saw the company was amply provided with convicts. . . . I don't mind saying that for many years the company found it to be an effective club over the heads of the free miners." [5]

In 1926 legislation to abolish the lease system in Alabama was defeated largely because certain industrial interests insisted that the law must allow convicts to be used in emergencies such as strikes.

During 1928, in a molders' strike at Nashville, Tennessee, convicts were put to making stoves and doing foundry work. Finding that they were not getting enough production in that way, the stove companies arranged to have the convicts paroled into the outside plants. Several men were actually so paroled as strike-breakers. There have been many other such cases; but such incidents are often kept out of the press.

CHAPTER IV

"MAKING GOOD CITIZENS"

ONE of the most important factors determining penal methods in every capitalist country and especially in the United States is the desire to make profit out of the convicts. The claim that capitalist prisons are for the purpose of reforming convicts is ridiculous. In a recent speech before the American Prison Congress, Judge Andrew Bruce, professor of law at Northwestern University and a former judge of the Illinois Supreme Court, "declared that reform schools do not reform and prisons do not correct. He cited Al Capone as a product of the reform school." [1]

John McGivney, editor of the Tacoma (Washington) *Labor Advocate,* in a recent issue of his paper said: "In some states crime and criminals are being made a source of profit to such an extent that the herding of convicts, the imprisonment of human beings, has, in order to secure a labor supply for those profiteering states and firms, become quite an industry."

Howard B. Gill, superintendent of the State Prison Colony in Norfolk, Massachusetts, recently admitted: "During the 150 years which have elapsed since Vilain, the burgomaster of Ghent, erected his famous *Maison de Force* in 1771-1773, prison administrators, in America at least, have been more concerned with developing a profitable system than in directing it toward the reformation of the individual."

The "vocational" training given prisoners is often worthless. Garment making—especially work clothes—for instance, is the largest prison industry. The types of garments made in prison are practically all made on the outside by women. So a man may make shirts in prison for 20 years and yet not learn a thing that will help him earn a living when he gets out.

PRISON WAGES

One would suppose that if the idea of rehabilitation entered at all into this country's prison program the prisoners would get some reward, possibly wages, for their hard work. But 10 states pay nothing at all; a few give a small bonus as compensation for doing more than the allotted task. In other states a small weekly or monthly wage is paid, which in 65% of the cases is below 25 cents a day and is frequently less than five cents a day.

On this point, the Wickersham Commission reports:

It should be remembered that wages either have not been paid in our prisons or if paid have, with very few exceptions, been of negligible significance. Existing wage payments have been made still more negligible by a system of fining prisoners for violation of prison rules. There are cases on record in the state of New York in which prisoners who earned one and a half cents a day were fined five dollars at a time.[2]

In her study, *Welfare of Prisoners' Families in Kentucky*,[3] Ruth S. Bloodgood found that the "actual amount of money sent to the families was pitifully small as compared with their needs." She showed that the most the family of a prisoner might expect to receive from a prisoner regularly employed during the entire year was $23.40. This would be true if the father's entire year's earnings were sent to the family. But out of such earnings the prisoner had to buy certain necessities. Out of 82 families studied, 26 received less than $10 each. Only seven families received as much as $20.

But in addition to the money "wages" the prisoners receive other "rewards." For doing their work well, the most efficient workmen, according to the testimony of Tennessee convicts, are denied their paroles when due! The speedy workers are valuable both as producers and pace-setters and the contractors see to it that the parole applications of these men are rejected, even when the prisoner is eligible for parole. In Tennessee, in 1931, Parole Officer J. C. Acuff of Nashville admitted that he had embezzled funds collected under the parole provisions which require prisoners to pay $2 a month to the state to be held until the prisoners are released.

But Tennessee is not alone in such parole practices. In a recent hearing before the Committee on Labor of the House of Representatives members brought out that many men were "refused parole because they worked too well." Just a few months ago Benny Sabbatino, an ex-convict in the Great Meadow Prison, Comstock, New York, won an award of $7,500 against two former members of the parole board who kept him in prison three years beyond his time.[4]

Accidents and Occupational Diseases

An absolute lack of care in protecting the life and limb of convict slaves is one of the outstanding features of prison practice in this country. Fire hazard is one of the most serious dangers under which prisoners work. In the Ohio Penitentiary at Columbus, for example, 318 prisoners were cremated in less than an hour, when fire raged through it, April 21, 1930. Incidentally, the prison housed at the time 4,300 prisoners and was designed for but 1,500. On March 7, 1931, eleven Negro prisoners died screaming in agony when flames swept the prison at Kenansville, N. C. An "investigation" after the criminal tragedy revealed that it was known all along that the prison was a fire trap. In Coral Gables, Florida, in 1931, one convict was burned to death and several maimed for life in a serious fire.[5] Another of the most serious fires of the country's prison history was that in the Banner mines in Alabama in April, 1911. In this fire 123 prisoners, leased as coal miners to a private company, and all of them at work on the job, were killed like vermin.

Accident hazard is also prevalent in all prisons. In the

Brushy Mountain coal mine prison at Petros, Tennessee, for example, between 1928 and 1930, there were 42,854 hospital cases among less than 800 prisoners at any one time. An official investigating committee of Tennessee reporting on the Brushy Mountain Penitentiary in 1931 said that if a fire should break out in the prison, which it thought likely, a tragedy would occur "the like of which has probably never been seen in an American prison."

Occupational disease usually gets the prisoners who escape being burned to death or maimed by accident. The jute mill in San Quentin Prison, California, is one of the most hated of all prison factories. More has been written about it, possibly, than any other. A guard recently told a newspaper man who was visiting Tom Mooney, "They don't last long in the jute mill. Jute gets into the lungs and causes pulmonary trouble. After one year their health is broken." Tuberculosis is one of the most feared of all these prison diseases.

There is no recourse in law or anywhere else for prisoners or their families in cases of accident, disease or death. The courts have often held that in the absence of statutory provision, the state is not liable for injuries sustained by a convict working outside or inside the place of imprisonment. These same decisions hold that in the absence of a statute there is no liability to a prisoner who becomes diseased or who dies as a result of unhealthy conditions in a penal institution. These decisions are based on practical considerations, for otherwise many of the states would face "innumerable suits involving the injuries of prison inmates, so precarious are the conditions of the penal institutions, especially the road camps of the South." [6] Courts in New York, a state with so-called model prisons, have ruled likewise.

Only three states—Maryland, Wisconsin, and New Hampshire—have any sort of workmen's compensation for convicts. The compensation in these states is based on the "wages" received by the convict laborers which at best are a few cents a day. Then from this meager compensation are legally deducted charges of various sorts—board, maintenance and other items. Very little, if anything, is left for the prisoner. The law is much more interested in protecting the prison against loss because of disabled workers than in protecting the workers against disability.

HOURS AND TASKS

Convicts in the southern states are usually worked from 10 to 12 or even more hours a day. In some of them, especially on the chain gangs and farms, the hours are measured by the sun. "We work from sun to sun," is the way the prisoners express it, which means that work begins at daybreak and ends at sundown. But hours are long also in the central prisons or penitentiaries of the South. An official in the Nashville prison has often been heard to laugh and say, "Oh, yes, we work our men eight hours a day—eight hours before noon and eight after." This is the "full day" which this prison reports to investigators.

In prisons in northern states and other sections of the country, where the most efficient methods of prison labor exploitation have been worked out, the day's work is frequently as low as eight or nine hours.

The task system is common to all prisons in the United States—North, South, East and West. It is the "outside" system of piecework and speed-up transplanted into prisons. In a certain number of hours a prisoner is required to do a certain amount of work. As it is developed in the more efficient prisons it becomes similar to the "belt" or "line" in a Ford plant. The task is set by a skilled pace-setter. It is the same for all prisoners, skilled and unskilled. Each worker is then required to do that amount of work each day. Among the devices used to insure that he not only "does task" but exceeds it is a bonus for overproduction. This bonus consists of petty favors such as a small bag of smoking or chewing tobacco or stamps, or, in some cases, a few cents a week extra.* Another device is torture.

Punishment

All who have made the slightest study of prison labor know that throughout the country the great majority of prison punishments—from 75 to 90% of the cases—are given for not doing task.

After an extensive survey of prison-labor conditions, Kate Richards O'Hare reported: "If the women convicts failed to make task, and all of them did fail more or less, they were punished with fiendish cruelty—beaten, starved, frozen in winter, roasted in summer, strung up by the wrists with handcuffs, gagged, subjected to beastly sex perversion, and left to rot in dungeons." A prominent leader in the Alabama League of Women Voters recently told the writer that women tuberculars in Alabama prisons were flogged when they failed to do enough work or when their work did not suit the officials.

Warden A. A. McCorkle of Nashville prison admitted to the Tennessee legislative investigating committee in 1931 that he frequently ordered men given as high as 30 to 40 blows with a heavy strap "as a last resort for not pulling task."

A Tennessee convict, Harry Good, who was released from the Nashville prison in December, 1930, told of his experiences in that "reform institution." "I saw a friend of mine," he said, "taken to the whipping room. I heard him scream for half an hour. When he came to the hospital where I was confined, his back was bleeding and all the flesh had been torn away. His clothing stuck to torn and jagged flesh."

To escape the inhuman punishment meted out for inability to do the required quota of work, men frequently mutilate

* Prison labor contractors have also been known to supply "dope" to convicts to get more work out of them. *Cf.* E. Stagg Whitin, *Penal Servitude*, p. 79.

their bodies. In this way they gain sanctuary, for a time at least, in the hospital. Workers in Alabama mines, up until 1928, frequently put dynamite caps in their boots and blasted off toes or feet, or attached the caps to fingers and then smashed them with a rock. When the officials found too many such cases, they discouraged it by giving the men severe lashings as soon as they were partially recovered from their injuries.

Harry Good, the Tennessee convict, told of a friend of his who was being driven insane by the toil and monotony of the treadmill labor in the shirt factory. The friend told Good, "I borrowed a hatchet, laid my hand on the block and off came John Thumb—it didn't hurt much. Anyway, it was worth it." Another of his fellow-convicts, who worked in a foundry, poured molten lead into his shoe and had to keep his leg in plaster of Paris for several weeks and ended up a cripple.

George Bricker, ex-prisoner in the Brushy Mountain coal mine prison, spoke of his experiences with the task system. He said: "It has not been told how four strong men are called in to hold a man to the floor while he is lashed with a nine-pound whip for 'infraction of rules,' and 'infraction of rules' usually means failure to get task . . . I was whipped three times, each time receiving 15 to 27 lashes for 'not getting task'."

Tennessee is not the only state that has such conditions in its prisons. The writer simply happens to be more familiar with the situation in that state. In other states conditions are found to be practically the same. For example, in San Quentin, where Tom Mooney has rotted away over 16 years of his life, and in Folsom Prison, where his fellow frame-up victim, Warren K. Billings, is incarcerated, men are kept in solitary confinement in dungeons on a few ounces of bread and water for 11 days at a time and longer. And lime is spilled over the floor of the dungeon, giving off a suffocating odor. Prisoners claim that this punishment is given for not performing task.

Details of fiendish tortures at the Wichita, Kansas, Prison Camp continue to seep out despite the denials by those in charge of the farm. Failure to perform forced labor either because of sickness, weakness or any other cause is punished by bread and water rations and a 50% reduction of the credit given for working out fines. One prisoner, Peter J. Gentile, who had been kept on bread and water for 35 days, was recently taken into the potato field to work. He was too weak to hoe and started for the shade. A guard attacked him and with a blackjack scalped a long piece of skin from Gentile's head.

A short time ago tales of torture of convicts working in the Connecticut State Prison at Wethersfield, became a national scandal when Miss Genevieve Cowles, engaged for several years painting murals in the prison chapel, and Chaplain William H. Smith exposed conditions there.[7]

Miss Cowles is convinced that prison slavery tends to turn men into criminals. In her report on the Wethersfield prison she said that under the Connecticut statutes, Section 1978, revised 1930, "the warden is authorized in case prisoners are disobedient or disorderly or do not faithfully perform their tasks to put fetters and shackles on them or confine them in dark and solitary cells." These cells, called "Black Holes," each have two metal doors with a few slots as big as dollars for "ventilation." There are no mattresses in the punishment cells.

Chaplain Smith likewise charges that slavery exists in the Wethersfield prison. He says, "Like slaves you go to your task; the monotonous routine deadens your faculties; utter helplessness makes you rebellious; the ceaseless repression drives you frantic." Both Miss Cowles and Mr. Smith declare that driving and merciless labor accounts, in part, for dozens of mental cases in the cell blocks.

Prison "Home" Life

The preceding paragraphs on conditions tell of convicts toiling on the job. But what of their "home" conditions? Surely when their day's heavy toil is over, when their long hours of exploitation are ended, they should come back to good food, a nice rest under pleasant surroundings, and good treatment—all of which should characterize a real "reform" institution.

But that would cost money and decrease the profits of this capitalist institution. Actually one finds that convict laborers are given not only an insufficient amount of the cheapest food obtainable, but even this is usually badly prepared. A former convict in a Tennessee prison says that "not once during the time I served in Nashville prison were the prisoners, outside the hospital, given butter or milk." Another convict, describing a southern prison, declares, "we were sent into the mines on food which consisted of half-done rice, water gravy and old corn bread, which was our breakfast every day in the week. When we wanted anything else we had to cook it in our shovels, dirty and filthy with coal dust. Rusty water we had to drink if we could get it before the mine mules did." One Alabama county makes the boast that it is much cheaper to feed its convicts than its mules—it costs 55 cents a day for a mule and only 14 for a convict! And food allowances for convicts all over the country have been cut sharply during the economic crisis just as wages have been cut and living standards of workers reduced on the "outside." Sing Sing recently reduced its allowance 10% and at present 23 cents a day is allowed each convict for food. Prisons, like other capitalist institutions, increase profits at the expense of the workers.

When the Tennessee investigating committee was inspecting the Brushy Mountain Penitentiary they found 138 sufferers from influenza and pneumonia among the 800 prisoners in the place. No attempt was made to segregate the sick from the well. The committee reported: "They have a little shack called the pest house, which would not possibly accommodate more than three beds and that was not even in use." It was reported recently that on a single prison farm in Mississippi there were 19 cases of spinal meningitis arising out of unsanitary conditions. It is an established fact that in few, if any, of the prisons of the country is there an adequate system of physical examination and segregation and treatment of such contagious diseases as tuberculosis, gonorrhea, syphilis, trachoma, influenza and others.

Another "home" condition forced upon Tennessee convict-miners was described by the official committee in 1931: "Sodomy is practiced promiscuously. The younger prisoners are often forced to submit to the hardened old types." A well-informed labor official of Tennessee told the writer that these conditions of sex perversion exist with the knowledge and connivance of prison officials who assign "gal-boys" to model, hard-working prisoners. Of all the prisoners in the institution 60% were found to be infected with loathsome venereal diseases. "Many young boys," reported the Committee, "are infected with gonorrhea and syphilis." The venereals are not segregated but work alongside the other prisoners and use the same wash basins, towels and beds.

It is a well-known fact—though not agreeable and therefore not often mentioned—that sex perversion of the type described in Tennessee exists in every prison in the United States. A few years ago a deputy warden of the Federal penitentiary at Leavenworth was indicted for practicing sodomy on inmates of that prison.[8]

STRAIT-JACKET AND OTHER TORTURES

For the slightest sign of revolt against these working conditions prisoners are subjected to all sorts of tortures. At least eight states legalize the lash and many more use it though it is "illegal." In addition we find such torture instruments and "disciplinary punishments" as the stocks, solitary confinement on bread and water, confinement in "sweat boxes," hanging on cell walls, drenching with cold water, and many others.   But of all tortures none has been so well described as the strait-jacket.   Jacob Oppenheimer, former prisoner in San Quentin, gives his experiences with it:

I had not been in it fifteen minutes when sharp, needle-like pains began shooting through my fingers, hands and arms, which gradually extended to my shoulders . . . within half an hour these pains shot back and forth like lightning. Cramping pains clutched my bowels; my breath pained with a hot dry sensation. The brass rivets ate into my flesh, and the cord ground into my back until the slightest movement, even breathing, was an added agony. My head grew hot and feverish, and a burning thirst seized me which compelled me every few minutes to ask the guard for water. . . . As the hours and days passed the anguish became more and more unbearable.   I slept neither night nor day. . . . The bodily excretions over which I had no control in the canvas vice, ate into my bruised limbs, adding pain to pain. My fingers, hands and arms finally became numb and a paralyzing shock stunned my brain. . . .

Had I been offered a dose of poison I would have drunk it with gratitude. This I suffered for 4 days and 14 hours incessantly. . . . Released, I reeled off to my cell where I sank on my mattress in utter collapse. . . . I managed to drag off my saturated clothes. . . . What a sight I beheld. My hands, arms and thigh were frightfully bruised and had all the colors of the rainbow. My body was shriveled like that of an old man and a horrible stench arose from it.[9]

In order to cover up and distract attention from such conditions which prevail for convicts both while on the job and during rest hours, various publicity-seeking prison officials give the convicts a treat about once a year.   These treats include entertainments of various sorts—turkey dinners, speeches by social workers, movie stars and so on.   The latest scheme is to have football games. Thus the New York *Times,* November 18, 1931, carried an editorial praising Sing Sing's football eleven. But less than two weeks later the same paper reported that additional tear gas equipment was being sent to the Great Meadow Prison (in the same state) and that 30 additional guards had been requested by Warden Joseph H. Wilson.

Young Convict Workers

It is not only adult prisoners who are subject to daily abuses. Juvenile delinquent workers in American prisons also undergo maltreatment and even torture, and fatal consequences are often reported. Writing of conditions in the Washington State Reformatory at Monroe, the Wickersham Commission's investigator, Dr. Miriam Van Waters, said: "Punishment in the dark cells is given for trivial as well as serious offenses: not standing at count, speaking in the dining room, laughing in the cell block, making loud popping noises with the mouth, were listed on some of the discipline slips of the federal cases studied." Dr. Van Waters was told by a member of the staff of one reformatory that a young prisoner was found dead in one of the punishment cells.

Concerning the industrial reformatory at Chillicothe, Ohio, Dr. Van Waters charged that "a few minor offenses noted in the records as punished by from three to six days in the guard house were possession of a two-cent stamp, talking in mess line, concealing an apple in the bunk, kicking a refuse can, stealing five eggs from the kitchen."

During the six months ending December, 1930, there were 2,243 boys and girls under 18 in federal prisons. (The Wickersham report did not deal with the vast number of state and local delinquents.) Of this number 44.2% were in for violation of liquor laws. Eighteen were under 14 years of age.

Many children are doing long sentences at hard labor also in state institutions. Julian Leavitt some years ago reported that in the Greendale House of Reform in Kentucky, 200 children under 15 were leased out at three cents an hour to the Kentucky Furniture Co., a subsidiary of the Ford-Johnson Co. of Cincinnati.

The Tennessee legislative investigating committee in 1931 investigated also some boys' and girls' reformatories, including one for Negro children. It was found that these children were contracted out to private establishments. Salant and Salant Mfg. Co., shirt manufacturers of New York, were using most of the prisoners in the State Agricultural and Training School for Boys at Nashville where the youthful inmates are beaten for not "pulling task."

Governor Charles W. Tobey of New Hampshire in July, 1930, charged that young girls working in the State Industrial School at Manchester were given the "whipping cure" of over a hundred lashes apiece on their naked bodies. Some of the girls were also found confined in boxes covered with chicken wire.

Women prisoners in the United States are not treated with any more consideration than work animals. A part of the Tennessee investigating committee's report in 1931 dealt with treatment of women convict workers. It declared that "In the Nashville penitentiary in the women's building women are required to work in a hosiery mill and certain tasks are assigned to them. We found women being handcuffed and hung on pegs. . . . The inmates state that this was done for failure to perform task." The women testified that they were frequently left hanging for 10 hours. We have already referred to the flogging of tubercular women in Alabama prisons for not doing enough work. There are also instances of the strait-jacket and solitary confinement being used on women. At the New York State Reformatory for Women, Bedford Hills, New York, women inmates unaccustomed to heavy work were required to put up fences, clear ground and pour concrete.

Revolts and Struggles Against Prison Labor

The American Federation of Labor has opposed only that part of prison labor which turns out products made by its skilled craft unions. This policy was summarized in the statement of President William Green at the A. F. of L. convention in 1931 to the effect that it is "satisfactory" for prison laborers to make bricks but not to lay them. In other words, the A. F. of L. will oppose prison labor only when it does work of the same kind as that performed by the craft unions that make up the federation.

Although the A. F. of L. has done little or nothing to fight for better conditions for the workers in the prisons of this country, the latter, on their own initiative, have waged some bitter struggles against the conditions we have outlined in this chapter. In some cases these prison revolts have been aided by workers on the outside who were acting in their own interest as well as out of sympathy for their imprisoned and victimized fellow-workers.

Leased or bound-out prisoners were in most of the revolts of indentured servants, convicts and slaves before the Revolutionary War. Since then they have engaged in many fights. In the period from 1881 to 1900, for example, there are 22 recorded strikes against convict labor in coal mines.[10] Most of them have been forgotten as very few records were kept, or because the whole matter was hushed up by the ruling class at the time it occurred.

Perhaps the most significant of all such revolts was the Coal Creek Rebellion in 1891-92 in the coal mines of East Tennessee. Following a combination lock-out and strike, convict strike-breakers were brought in by the Tennessee Coal, Iron & Railroad Co. (now a subsidiary of the United States Steel Corp.), which leased an average of 1,500 to 1,600 convicts from the State of Tennessee. The company paid to the state an average of $42 a year for the use of an able-bodied worker. Naturally with such cheap labor power huge profits were piled up. It may be said that this company was built upon the trade and exploitation of convict slaves.

The president of the corporation at that time was Thomas C. Platt, Republican boss of New York in the 1890's. Members of the New York legislature and other northern capitalists owned stock in the company. However, the convicts were bound out to Mr. Platt, the Republican, by the southern Democratic legislature and governor of Tennessee.

The miners, Negro and white, aided by the farmers of East Tennessee, drove out the guards, burned the prison stockades throughout East Tennessee and released the convicts who escaped to the hills. Governor Buchanan sent in the militia to subdue the workers. After a pitched battle the entire force of soldiers was captured and driven out after being disarmed and after promising never to return to the mining section. The struggle had begun in earnest. It lasted from July 14, 1891 (Bastille day), to November, 1892, with a few skirmishes as late as 1893.

Before the struggle was over nearly a dozen prisons were burned to the ground and over 1,000 convicts given their freedom, food and clothing. Many convicts chose to remain and fight, risking recapture. Most of them escaped into the hills of Kentucky, West Virginia and North Carolina, and were never recaptured.

Three commanding officers, a general, a colonel and a captain were captured as well as several hundred soldiers, including whole train loads at a time. Many of the soldiers were very easy to "capture" as they openly sided with the miners and convicts. Even the United States War Department was forced to admit that most of the people of Tennessee, "including the militia," were in sympathy with the miners.

Negroes and whites, men who fought for the North and men who fought for the South in the Civil War, farmers and miners, convicts and "free" men, stuck together in the face of the entire armed forces of Tennessee. Approximately 10,000 soldiers and members of business men's posses were used to crush the revolt. Workers and convicts stormed forts and cannons and died together. But they died with the knowledge that they had killed a great many more of the common enemy than the enemy killed of them. Over 500 miners were arrested after the workers had been disarmed.

Before the lease system was adopted in Tennessee, in 1889, convicts were worked under contract for private contractors at Nashville. But after the convicts burned the prison on several occasions and with it all the manufactured goods in the place, the employers repudiated their contracts. It was then that the convicts were leased to the coal mines.

The 1931 Tennessee legislative committee in its report on conditions in Tennessee prisons referred to the Coal Creek Rebellion and declared that unless conditions are improved similar trouble would be expected in connection with the state-owned prison coal mine at Brushy Mountain.

STRUGGLES IN 1931-32

Revolts and strikes have broken out in prisons all over the United States during 1931 and 1932. Many of them were not reported, or if reported were "played down" or called "riots." There were strikes in at least three reformatories for girls in the South and the institutions were wrecked or burned. The two most important of these fights occurred at the Samarcand "House of Correction" near Charlotte, N. C., where 350 revolted and at the Alabama "Training School for Girls," near Birmingham. There were many riots in other sections of the country.

The most important chain gang strike in 1931 occurred in Loudon County, Tennessee. The Negro and white convicts there asked for an 8-hour day and better food. Two guards quit in sympathy.[11] In July, 1932, seventy convicts on the Sunbeam prison chain gang in Florida went on strike against brutal conditions and won a transfer.

On December 13, 1931, the boiler crew in Leavenworth refused to work. Two strikes were reported in New Jersey in 1931. The most important occurred in the Reformatory at Rahway, August 24. Striking to raise their wages to four cents a day—they had been three cents—the prisoners

defied the officials. All convicts were locked in their cells and
deprived of any sort of exercise. About 50 of the most
active men were thrown in dungeons on bread and water.
Unemployed civilians were brought in as strike-breakers.
On August 31, the strike was broken and about half of the
816 striking convicts went back to work.

A strike occurred on a Richmond, Indiana, gang in February 23, 1932, when 800 workers on the gang protested
against a cut in wages which were paid in scrip and groceries.

Under a headline reading: "Attempted Use of Sweat-Box
Brings Prison Camp Strike," a Florida dispatch to the New
York *American,* October 28, 1932, reports the most recent
revolt of prison inmates. Continuing, the report speaks of
30 or 40 "white convicts at a road camp near Indiantown . . .
[who] have gone on strike and are being held at bay in a
fenced enclosure by guards and armed trusties." This State
Road Camp at Indiantown is also the place where two militant workers, Angel Carbrero and Ismael Cruz, Tampa political prisoners, are now confined.

Thus the convicts, in some cases helped by "free" workers,
have struggled against their exploiters. Thus far they have
fought without any plan or leadership, without any clear idea
of what they expected to accomplish. But now that the
class character of prison labor is being recognized and the
number of labor and political prisoners is increasing, such
plans, leadership and purposes will be developed. And it is
certain that many of the half million or so victimized and
imprisoned members of the working class will be among the
most militant fighters against capitalism. As immediate demands the militant labor movement will struggle to better
prison conditions; it will seek to expose the class character of
prisons; it will seek to secure equal pay for convicts doing
equal work with "free labor." It will seek to eliminate the
special concessions given prison contractors who, because of
low production costs—no taxes, fuel or rent—can undersell
the products of "free" workers.

Convict labor, one of the most lucrative sources of state and even private income, is thus accompanied by all the methods of force and brutality common to the exploitation of direct forced labor. And it leads to revolts just as the exploitation of "free labor" leads to strikes. The prison system in the United States is a specialized part of the whole system of capitalist exploitation and oppression, subjecting workers who are victimized by the more indirect system of labor exploitation when they are "outside," to even more direct and brutal forms of exploitation. Any illusion about "prison reform" in the capitalist penal structure should be completely dispelled by an examination of the chain gang, the special institution established by the Southern Bourbons to keep the masses—especially the Negro masses—in subjection.

CHAPTER V

THE CHAIN GANG

WORK on the chain gang, one of the chief penal institutions of the South, is the most brutal type of convict forced labor in the United States. The editor of the *Southern Worker* recently wrote: "Tsarist Russia had its Siberia; the Balkans has its underground inquisition; Venezuela its torture chamber; France its Devil's Island—and America its Chain Gang."

Historically speaking the chain gang has been largely an instrument with which to terrorize, torture and exploit Negroes. It was adopted on a grand scale at the end of the Civil War and was one of the devices consciously developed by the former slaveholders to put the newly "freed" Negroes back into bondage. Before the Civil War most convicts in the South were whites, but soon after the war this situation was reversed and Negro prisoners were in the overwhelming majority for many years.

During the past few years, however, the number of white prisoners on chain gangs has grown considerably. This may be attributed largely to the economic crisis and the chronic agricultural crisis since the World War, resulting in a further impoverishment of white as well as Negro workers and farmers, and an increase in petty property law violations.

When some of the inhuman tortures and murders that constantly occur on the gangs are forced into the light, reformers and liberal apologists for capitalism are "shocked" and call for investigation. The investigation usually whitewashes the prison system as a whole by pinning the blame on one or two subordinate guards who are dismissed. The reformers then go into ecstasy over their "victory."

In 1923 Martin Tabert, a young white convict, was

whipped to death in a privately owned lumber camp in Florida. When the news leaked out reformers and even state officials were horrified. To think of such conditions existing in the United States in 1923! An "investigation" was held. It resulted in the prosecution of a few prison guards and the "abolition" of whipping. This was considered a "victory"! But in 1932 the papers were full of the details of how Arthur Maillefert, a young New Jersey boy on a Florida chain gang, was whipped unmercifully and then placed in a sweat-box with a chain around his neck until he died. Where was the great "victory" of 1923? It had long since been forgotten. A Florida state official has recently been quoted as saying: "I read about this torture stuff happening a hundred years ago, but I never dreamed it could happen right here in America in this day and age." He evidently had never heard of the Martin Tabert case of 1923.

There have been other great "victories." A few years ago, after a series of particularly brutal chain gang murders were revealed in North Carolina, Governor O. Max Gardner abolished the lash by proclamation. The hats of the reformers sailed skyward as they cheered this liberal governor. But their silk top-pieces had barely been retrieved when Willie Bellamy, a frail Negro boy still in his teens, was whipped into unconsciousness and then placed in a sweat-box where he died.

These are but a few of the numerous cases which may be cited to show that the "victories" won by the reformers in securing "investigations" do not affect the prison system in any way. And in 8 southern states whipping is still openly legalized. The chain gang exists primarily to exploit labor and to terrorize workers on the outside into accepting their lot without complaining.

Chain gang prisoners are usually worked on the repair and construction of roads or similar public works for the state or for private contractors who profit richly from this super-exploitation of labor. It is reported that the state of

Georgia alone made a profit of $3,270,000 on the operation of chain gangs in four years.

The convict-slaves are usually hobbled with chains which they must wear at all times even while at work or asleep. The chains are riveted around the legs and can be removed only with a cold chisel on the prisoner's release from the gang. Hence the name "chain gang."

A vivid picture of how convicts live on a South Carolina chain gang is contained in *Georgia Nigger*, John L. Spivak's novel of peonage and chain gang life in the deep South.

In Buzzard's Roost [a Georgia chain gang—*W. W.*] there were vermin and stench, cursings and beatings and stocks but out of Slatternville seventeen Negroes went into the wilderness of the South Carolina hills in a floating cage, a cage drawn by four mules, a swaying, creaking, rumbling prison of thick wood with no bars or windows for air on nights that choked you, and bunks of steel with rungs for master chains to lock you in at night. Bedbugs slept with you in that cage and lice nestled in the hair of your body and you scratched until your skin bled and the sores on your body filled with pus. Meat for the floating kitchen wrapped in burlap bags, stinking meat swarming with maggots and flies, and corn pone soaked by fall rains, slashing rains that beat upon the wooden cage through the barred door upon the straw mattresses until they were soggy.

Gaunt-eyed convicts, stinking like foul creatures long buried in forgotten dungeons. . . .

Men toil on these gangs from sun to sun, from 10 to 14 hours a day, according to season. They are slaves without any capital value. Beaten and killed—it really doesn't matter to their masters. Other workers can be brought to take their places. The men slave at crushing rock, felling trees, building levees, digging ditches, building roads. Brutal guards with whips and guns watch to see that the stripe-clothed convicts work speedily and continuously. Blisters and sores from worn-out, ill-fitting shoes, and swollen, blistered, calloused hands are inevitable. Infections are frequent as a result.

Housing conditions in the chain gang camps are the worst imaginable. One form of house for the prisoners is a cage-like cell, mounted on wheels, so that it can be moved from place to place as the camp follows the jobs. The cage is about 13 feet long, 8 feet high, 7 feet wide, and looks more like a cage for ferocious animals than anything else in the world, except that the convict-animal cage is not gilded as are those of the animals in a circus. Such a cage is "home" for about 20 men. During the hot summer nights the men, packed sardine-like into this cage, sweat and stink, but rarely sleep. When night comes the tired workers come from work to find a piece of coarse, dirty cloth stretched over lumpy straw, usually alive with bugs. This is their bed.

All the men are forced to lie down on their bunks in rows. A long chain is then run through the short leg chains which are riveted to the legs of the men. Thus every man is securely fastened to every other man, and can't get out of the chain even to go to the toilet—a hole in the floor of the cage—without waking all the men on the chain. In case of fire the men are held together until unlocked from the long chain. In several cases fires, under such circumstances, have resulted in loss of life.

Another method of housing is in tents pitched on the ground near a creek or spring. Around both types of camps flies and mosquitoes swarm in clouds. Near by are uncovered sewerage pits. All convicts, venereals and tuberculars, sick and well, use the same wash basins, towels and beds. There is no attempt to segregate sufferers from contagious diseases, despite pretty-looking laws providing for such segregations.

Food for the chain gang victims is usually worse than in other types of prisons. It consists at best of corn bread and grits, grease gravy, beans, black coffee for one meal, occasionally salt pork, and infrequently vegetables of some sort.

The Guards Are Killers

The men in charge of the gangs are brutal and ignorant. Most of them have had experience as guards for private employers in turpentine camps, levee building jobs, or for other private peon exploiters. A prime qualification to get a job as a guard is to know how to "handle niggers and bloodhounds." It often happens that white convicts are made trusties and used to guard other convicts, especially Negroes. Frequently they are used to chase escaped prisoners with bloodhounds and guns. Sometimes a new prisoner, especially a Negro, who arrives in camp, not knowing the ropes, is encouraged to "escape" by trusties and other guards who hope to split the bond money or to get a reward or a pardon for recapturing or shooting the escaping prisoner. In Mississippi trusty-guards shot so many prisoners "trying to escape," that legislation had to be passed to stop the rewards.

The most notorious of these trusty-guards was Cecil Houston, known as the "Killer of Flat Top," an Alabama convict serving a life term for murder. A prison investigation in that state in 1926 revealed that this killer, together with others like him, was used to enforce the speed-up by the state and private coal companies which had leased the prisoners. It was proved that Houston killed several fellow prisoners and had broken both arms of at least seven others. His favorite method was to slip up behind an unsuspecting convict and with a heavy hickory pick-handle knock him cold. Then before his victim regained consciousness Houston would break both his arms, thereby preventing any resistance. The investigation revealed that 90% of the convicts examined exhibited scars, reminders of brutal taskmasters. These brutal methods were used primarily to make the prisoners work faster and produce more coal.

Houston was given a special bonus for all coal that was produced. By driving the men he was thus able to support his family in style on the outside and put money in the savings bank every month. Although imprisoned for murder he was given many special privileges. When the murders in the prison were exposed, Houston, who had helped commit them, was out in the city on a week's vacation!

MAN HUNTING

Man hunting has always been a favorite sport of the southern ruling class. Formerly the sport was in chasing escaped slaves; now it is in hunting escaped convicts—hunting "niggers" with bloodhounds. "Why, it's just like fox hunting," a guard declared, "and it gives the young dogs such valuable training, too." Several cases of guards using prisoners as a means of training dogs to hunt escaped prisoners have appeared in the press in spite of efforts to keep them quiet.

A prisoner who has incurred the displeasure of the guards is forced to get some distance ahead of the guard who is holding the dogs. Then the dogs are released and chase the prisoner who barely has time to take refuge up a tree. From the tree he is forced to tease the dogs who have "treed" him by throwing at them or striking them with a long pole.

When the guards feel that the dogs are savage enough the convict is forced to jump from the tree among them. If he is hesitant, the guards make him jump by shooting at him from a distance with small bird shot.

CHAIN GANG TORTURES

Punishment of chain gang slaves nine times out of ten is for not doing enough work—not keeping up with pacesetters. The punishment includes binding in cuffs and shackles, flogging (as high as 100 blows with a heavy leather whip), confinement in "dog houses" or sweat boxes, clubbing and binding in stocks which suspend the body by the legs and arms in the manner of stocks used in New England in the early days.

The sweat boxes are small coffin-like cells just large

enough to suspend a man in an upright position. A small hole the size of a silver dollar lets in the only air. The cell is placed in the hot tropic sun, or sometimes a metal plate underneath is heated with fire. It is one of the worst of all prison tortures.

In the appendix of documents and photographs to John L. Spivak's *Georgia Nigger* are shocking forms of torture witnessed and photographed by the author. An official report from Banks County, Georgia, dated September, 1931, records that one Grover Hammond was "put in barrel" for "disobeying guard." The use of iron halters around the necks of convicts is recorded in a photograph taken by the author in Muscogee County, Ga., and the use of spikes was photographed in Decatur County, Ga. Spivak describes them thus:

David sat on the ground and held first one foot and then the other on a block of wood while the spikes were being riveted. The eye between the two steel prongs fitted closely around the ankle, with just enough space for pants to be pulled through when changing clothes. The weight on his feet was heavy when he rose. With his first step the projections clashed noisily against each other.

"Spread yo' laigs," the blacksmith cautioned.

David gained the steps of the Negro cage walking straddle-legged. Spikes was the warden's answer to his mad effort to run away, steel to remind him at each step that he was marked for special attention, sharp points of steel, bayonets of steel before him and bayonets of steel behind him—because Chickasaw county wanted him to finish a road for a white planter.

These 20-pound weights permanently riveted around the legs are a drawn-out torture leading to exhaustion. During the day they rub against the legs, creating sores which often become infected. Such infections are known as "shackle poison." At night the convict's rest is repeatedly broken by the need of raising his legs whenever he turns in his bunk.

A form of torture the horror of which shocked the civilized world when it was inflicted in the Belgian Congo upon slaves, also is used in Georgia, and Spivak describes a convict undergoing it:

David saw him lying near the stocks in the blaze of sun, trussed up like a pig ready for slaughter. His head lay loosely on the red soil as though the neck had been broken. His eyes were closed. His legs and arms, tied with ropes, pointed to the sky, the whole body kept motionless by a pick thrust between the tied limbs. His mouth was open. The veins in his temples and arms stood out, swollen. And swarming over the face and arms and neck were myriads of tiny red ants.

But the extreme torture of breaking convicts on the Georgia rack, witnessed and photographed by Spivak is recorded both in pictures and a vivid description:

Through the bar figures could be seen moving silently and swiftly before the white post. The warden, an absurd figure in his underwear, held a flare high.

The unresisting Negro, with his back to the post, was laced to it from ankles to hips with a rope and the one tied to the cuffs slipped about the second post. The guard pulled sharply. The convict's torso jerked forward, bending at right angles, his arms outstretched. His head drooped between the arms. The sweat on his back and arms glistened in the light.

"Stretch!" the warden ordered harshly.

The guard pulled until the rope was as taut as a tuned violin string.

"Oh Jesus!" the Negro screamed. "Yo' pullin' my arms out!"

The rope was wound around the post and tied, leaving the convict stretched so the slightest movement threatened to wrench his shoulders from their sockets.

A committee of women investigating a prison camp in Alabama about two years ago used an order, authorizing the investigation by the Governor to compel guards to break open a sweat box. A man was suspended in it by the wrists. His weight was on his numbed arms. He was unconscious. Lime had been placed in the bottom of the box and had eaten into his feet, which were swollen to twice their natural size. When released the worker pitched forward on his face.

A good idea of torture can be had by analyzing conditions in a typical gang. In 1925 Nevin C. Cranford, a chain gang superintendent of a Stanley County, North Carolina,

gang was indicted on charges of murdering at least six prisoners. An investigating committee took sworn testimony
from many of the prisoners in the camp. Among the testimony we find such items as follows: Grady Sides, a prisoner,
stated that his wrist was broken while cranking a tractor;
that no surgical attention was given; that his arm was jerked
straight but not dressed; that no doctor saw him; that he
was made to continue at work with his broken arm hanging
useless at his side. D. Cage Hahn, a citizen, testified that
Cranford knocked a Negro prisoner into the creek while
he was heavily shackled and ordered two other prisoners to
jump in and drown him. Cranford admitted that he threw
Arthur Butler, Negro prisoner, into the creek. It was also
charged that Cranford made three prisoners hang William
Layton, another prisoner, by the heels with a steel wire for
two hours, blood streaming down into his face.

A complete sworn statement by one of the victims, Harold
Parks, gives a graphic picture of typical prison guards in
action. Parks swore:

That on the 26th day of June, 1924, he was tried in the County
Court of the aforesaid county, and convicted for an assault
with a deadly weapon, and sentenced to the chain gang for one
year. That he was driving a wheeler a short time thereafter
when a breast chain broke. He called Captain Cranford telling
him what had happened, he said I will fix that, ran up, began
to beat upon him with a large hickory stick four or five feet
long, an inch through, beat until he was all bloody, clothing
beat into strings, about that time some white men was coming
in sight. He, Crawford, ordered the affiant to get a feed sack,
cut an arm hole, and put it on like a coat so as to cover up
the bloody, tattered clothing. He received three more beatings
with a lash, 15 licks each time, cutting blood each lick, scars
all over the body, some scars yet.

At another time he saw the following: Arthur Butler (Negro)
was beaten with a leather strop almost every day, knocked down
with a big stick, beat on the ground, stomped, shot two times;
he was not doing a thing, hanged up by the wrist with sharp
wire for four hours until the blood would run down his arms;
then make to jerk until he got away; made to eat food with a

box of epson salts upon it when sick. If he got sick at the stomach and threw the food up (vomited) it was caught in a pan and he was made to eat it again, the Captain standing over him with his big whip. This man was treated worse than an animal.

Henry Wooten (Negro) was brought up to the camp late one evening. The first word Cranford said to him was, "Yes, you are the very man I have been wanting. I am going to get even with you. I will fix you. I have not forgot how big you drove past me when I was working on the New London road. You came near hitting some of the mules." The next day he knocked him down with a big hickory walking stick; beat him on the ground. This he did almost every day and at night or morning while in the camp. He would whip him with the big strop or buggy trace, until he had his back cut to pieces; after about two weeks he continued to beat him. Henry got so weak he could not work or walk. He would knock him down, stomp him. On one day he knocked him down and trampled him in the stomach and chest. The blood ran out of his mouth and nose. He could not do anything. Cranford got off some eight or 10 steps and took his pistol and shot several times through his hat and clothing to see if he, Henry, would move. He did not. Captain Cranford then ordered the tractor put in front, hitched it to his leg chains and would drag him over the rocks, stumps and bumps; his back was almost skinned. This was done many times. Afterwards the deceased, Henry Wooten, was stomped in the chest and stomach. He was never able to do anything or had he been able for many days before. But the blood continued to run out of his mouth and his bowels would not act, the food worked out of his mouth mingled with blood. This affiant waited upon the deceased for the last few days of his life. When he was not able to sit up and take his medicine, Captain Cranford stomped him for not getting up and beat him. For many days before he died his back and body was beaten into holes and they stunk so you scarce could stand it. His ankles where he had been double shackled were bad. The shackles had cut the skin and flesh to the leaders or tendons and his legs to his knees were swollen and bursted until they smelt bad. His last words was to me, he said, "I cannot live, I must die, I have been beaten to death, Cranford has killed me." And this affiant knows that he was beaten to death for no mortal man could stand what was inflicted upon this man.[1]

The prison doctor always helped the prison authorities cover up or whitewash such conditions. When Wooten died the doctor pronounced the cause of his death as "acute bowel trouble." Carl Meadows, a white prisoner who was also murdered by Cranford, was examined by the doctor and he too was found to have had "acute kidney trouble."

Witnesses in Cranford's trial testified that he once killed a prisoner, John Quincy Leake, and buried him secretly. The prison authorities and the state were responsible for such conditions just as much as Cranford. The state legalized the lash. G. D. Troutman, chairman of the road commission, told an investigator of the state Charities Board that he was satisfied as long as the men received the same treatment as mules. Both he and County Attorney W. E. Smith, said "the only way to appeal to a nigger is through his hide."

Many examples of such forced labor tortures could be cited. Cranford committed his tortures and murders in North Carolina in the years before 1925. The writer visited three Marion, North Carolina, textile strikers who were sentenced to the Hendersonville chain gang in 1930 for strike activities. "While it was so hot," one said, "the prisoners worked until they fell, completely exhausted. Then they were carried to the shade for a few minutes. If they were sick, they were allowed to stay in the shade until the doctor came; then if he ordered them to work they had to go or get whipped. I have heard strong men crying and begging for mercy as they were beaten with a heavy leather strap." This beating with a strap occurred long after Governor O. Max Gardner had issued an "order" for no more whipping! Soon afterwards Willie Bellamy, a young Negro convict on a Wake County gang, was whipped and clubbed and then smothered to death in a sweat box. But it was a "great victory" to have the Governor "abolish" whipping by proclamation.

A Few Killings

Toiling on the gangs men frequently die from sunstroke during the hottest summer days. More often, however, they are worked to death or shot or whipped until they die. In such cases the officials whitewash the real cause of death and conceal it in their reports by saying that such and such a prisoner died of "sunstroke," or merely "died of natural causes." Occasionally such cases crop up in the press. An unemployed Spanish-American War veteran was whipped to death on a Memphis, Tennessee, gang in 1932. The cause of his death was reported as "a blocked artery," but the undertaker discovered evidence of a terrible flogging. Odell Johnson, a 19-year-old Augusta, Georgia, youth, died on a Greenwood, South Carolina, gang from "sunstroke" in July, 1931. Later fellow prisoners charged that he was murdered and Governor Ibra C. Blackwood ordered an "investigation."

Thomas Farmer, a young convict in a Georgia prison camp, died from a "heat stroke" in 1931. Later it was brought out that Farmer was maltreated, including being chained to a post and left while sick. In June, 1931, Cecil Lafferty, 17-year-old inmate of a Boonesville, Missouri, prison camp, died as a result of a beating. Delph C. Simons, director of penal institutions, said the preliminary investigation indicated that Lafferty was whipped because he was "stalling" while at work in the field.

In 1932 a big scandal came to light in Alabama when a disabled World War veteran, James C. Kirby, was severely beaten by a heavy leather whip on the Ardmore prison gang. His crime was failure to work hard enough. Kirby said he was unable to perform the strenuous gang work because of having been gassed in the war. He had been fined $25 for trespassing—probably walking along a railroad track—but when court costs were added he owed the county a total of $85. To pay the fine and costs he had to serve 101 days at hard labor. After an "investigation" Governor B. M. Miller declared that "neither the law nor prison regulations had been violated in *whipping* Kirby" for not working hard enough. Thus the Governor frankly admitted that the whipping torture is legal.

One of the most recent chain gain scandals comes from Florida where Arthur J. Maillefert, 19-year-old youth from New Jersey, was severely beaten and then hung in a sweat box by a trace chain until he choked to death. Before being whipped and placed in the sweat box young Maillefert had been stripped naked and placed in a barrel which had strips nailed across it so that the prisoner was locked in, though with legs and head protruding. The Sunbeam prison camp where he was confined is in the heart of mosquito-infested swamps.

Governor Doyle E. Carlton, who was a member of the Florida legislature which passed the law legalizing peonage, publicly defended the prison system after this killing. He said that the incident is "a rare exception in the prison life of Florida. . . . On the whole our prisoners are well cared for and well treated." But prisoners in Florida chain gangs, who should know, talk differently. Michael Tansey, a former Florida prisoner, for example, said:

I was riding a freight in Florida at the time. I was heading for a job picking oranges along with a lot of others. We were arrested outside of Tallahassee, Florida, when the train stopped and we were sentenced to from 90 days to eight months in the camp.

We were sent to the swamps to do logging and lay rails. After 24 hours there we prayed for death. . . . If we did not work fast enough we were whipped cruelly. The louder a man screamed the more lashes he got. If we could keep quiet we would get off with 15 or 20. And after beating us all week, Higginbotham [guard captain] and his guards would come around on Sunday and make us sing and dance for them.

Another prisoner, James Travis, described the treatment Maillefert received before his death. He said that in beating

Maillefert guard captain George W. Courson, a 200-pound man, had used a heavy "air hose" and then had knocked the youth down, although he was helplessly bound with shackles and "spur." Courson had wielded the air hose with both hands and with great force, according to Travis. When asked if a doctor had been called to treat Maillefert for the injuries inflicted upon him, Travis replied: "You don't get no doctor in them camps when you get beat up." Travis exhibited an ugly scar on his head, the result of treatment by guards, and declared that he had been ruptured by two guards kicking him. Pointing to his right ear, he said: "They smashed the side of my head with a pine sapling and now I'm deaf in this ear."

Another prisoner, William Roberts, testified that he had seen 15 or 20 men whipped in prison camps in Florida. Thus in spite of what the Governor said prison brutalities are common in Florida's prison gangs. The prison reformers having won a "great victory" in 1923 promptly forgot about prison horrors until the Maillefert case demonstrated that conditions to-day are just as bad as they were ten years ago. And it is not only in Florida that such prison conditions are found; they exist in almost every chain gang in the South.

In Florida prison camps and chain gangs in 1932 there were 11 of the 14 Tampa prisoners who were imprisoned for terms ranging from one to ten years for helping to organize workers into the Tobacco Workers Industrial Union. These prisoners have received particularly brutal treatment because they were militant workers. Some have been put through the sweat box. One of them, J. E. McDonald, serving 10 years on the Raiford chain gang, has received the worst treatment. After a month of torture he lost 30 pounds. His lips were blistered from fever and his ruddy complexion was sallow. Although recently having passed through an appendicitis operation, he was forced to push a plow all day long under the boiling sun.

The threat of a year on the chain gang hangs over all organizers of the Communist Party and Trade Union Unity League in Birmingham, Alabama. There the police arrested organizers (who were employed by their organizations and received wages for their work) and charged them with vagrancy which carries a sentence of one year on the chain gang. One Negro organizer in Chattanooga was rushed to the county chain gang after being convicted on a political charge before an appeal against the sentence could be filed, although intention to do so was declared at the trial. His release was forced by the International Labor Defense and the sentence defeated. One organizer was arrested while asleep in his hotel room by city detectives in Birmingham and charged with vagrancy!

PRISON FARM TORTURES

On the big prison farms, especially in Arkansas, Mississippi, Louisiana and Texas, failure to "do task," and the punishments for it, so closely resembles the chain gang—indeed the men are often worked in chains—that no special attention will be given them other than to mention conditions on a few typical farms.

In May, 1931, Mrs. W. A. Montgomery, head of Mississippi's prison trustee board, reported that an entire gang of convicts, picking cotton, were thrown across the rows and lashed because they complained to visiting trustees that they were not getting water enough while working. She reported also that a new prisoner, a bookkeeper in civil life (vocational training!), and suffering from a chronic illness, was forced to pick cotton until he died in the field with a cotton sack about his neck. The reported cause of his death was that common chain gang illness, "blocked artery."

Here is a case within the writer's personal knowledge. In 1926, Wiley Zeigler, a white railroad worker and union man, was whipped and spurred to death by a mounted guard on the prison farm near Houston, Texas. The writer saw

Zeigler's body as it lay in the morgue. His back was criss-crossed with long, deep, bloody cuts. On his neck were many tiny holes made by the rowel of the guard's spurs. Ill and unused to farm work, Zeigler had failed to get "on the row"—keep up while hoeing cotton under the hot Texas sun. The Houston *Press* in April, 1932, uncovered the grewsome story of how a Texas convict, A. D. Swor, was beaten to death on the Eastham Prison Farm, Hardin County, six years after the "investigation" and trial over Zeigler's death.

To serve one's sentence on these prison gangs and prison farms does not always mean that one has been completely "reformed," according to the *Handbook of American Prisons and Reformatories* for 1929. In Georgia, for example, "men are turned loose without any cash and given a railroad ticket to the point from which they were sentenced. On arrival without funds or jobs they are subject to arrest as vagrants by the police force and to trial by court officials who are paid on the fee basis for conviction."

The chain gang, the peculiar penal institution of the South, has its setting in that part of the country which has remained predominantly agrarian and where the Negroes are bound by the chains of the semi-feudal tenant system to big white landowners. Its brutality is an inevitable concomitant to the system of super-exploitation whose victim is the Negro people. Super-exploitation needs super-oppression to keep its victims in "their place." The chain gang serves as a weapon to enforce white ruling class domination and peonage, of which we shall have more to say in the next chapter.*

* For a succinct and graphic description of chain gang conditions, see John L. Spivak, *On the Chain Gang*, International Pamphlets, No. 32.

CHAPTER VI

PEONAGE

In addition to the use of convicts there are other systems of forced labor in the United States. The most widespread is peonage, involving as it does many thousands of workers and farmers, chiefly Negroes. It is especially prevalent in the South where planters and employers developed it as a substitute for the kind of slavery which was abolished with the Civil War. Indeed, peonage is nothing more than a concomitant of the tenant farming system which was deliberately and carefully established by the southern ruling class to perpetuate slavery under a different name. This tenant system is in many respects worse than the slavery it succeeded, for it combines absolute dependency on the part of the tenant with very little responsibility on the part of the landlord.

Before "freedom" the slaves lived in cabins back of the "big house" and toiled in the fields for their masters. After the Civil War they lived in the same cabins, picked cotton in the same fields—which often belonged to the same masters—and suffered practically all the evils of chattel slavery. For although the Negro demanded, and was even promised for a time by his northern allies, "40 acres of land and a mule," he never obtained the land which he had tilled in slavery and which should have been his if emancipation was to mean anything. Without land the freedman was in a completely dependent position and at the mercy of his former master or some other employer.

During the first two years after the Civil War the defeated slaveholders made their first onslaught against the newly freed Negro. During this period southern legislatures met. They passed a series of restrictive measures generally known as the Black Codes. These included vagrancy laws, laws against a worker breaking his contract, laws regulating employment agencies, the employment and migration of Negroes, apprenticeship laws for Negro children, and pauper laws—all aimed at securing a supply of forced labor in place of slavery. Each law was flexible enough to include tenant farmers, farm laborers, and industrial workers During the intervention of Federal troops these laws were not enforced for a brief period, but by 1877 they were again in force, and with the help of the Ku Klux Klan and methods of terror * the Negroes were thrust into a new bondage—peonage.

WHAT IS PEONAGE?

The term "peonage" is now generally applied in the United States to any method by which a person is physically or legally held in involuntary servitude, with the exception, of course, of convict labor. The Supreme Court has called it, "A status or condition of compulsory service, based upon the indebtedness of the peon to the master."

The operation of peonage in the case of tenant farmers ** or farm laborers is fairly typical of peonage in all industries. In 1919 the Memphis *Commercial-Appeal* carried a letter from a southerner which gives a good description of it:

In certain parts of the South, men who consider themselves men of honor and would exact a bloody expiation of the one who would characterize them as common cheats do not hesitate to boast that they rob the Negroes by purchasing their cotton at prices that are larcenous, by selling goods to them at extor-

---

* Lynching as a widely used ruling class weapon dates from this period. The *World Almanac* for 1932 gives the figure of 4,308 persons lynched from 1885 to 1930. These are recorded lynchings. Many are not recorded. See *Lynching*, by Harry Haywood and Milton Howard, International Pamphlets, No. 15.

** The term "tenant farmer" is used here to include all tenants—those that pay a certain amount of cash for the use of land, known as renters, and those who give a share of the crop for the use of the land, the share croppers.

tionate figures, and even by padding their accounts with a view of keeping them always in debt. A protest from a Negro against tactics of this kind is met with a threat of force. Justice at the hands of a white jury in sections where this practice obtains is inconceivable. Even an attempt to carry the matter into the courts is usually provocative of violence.[1]

This letter describes how a landlord "buys" the tenant's share of the crop and how he gets the tenant in his debt. The process is somewhat as follows: A contract is made between a tenant and a landlord. Customarily a provision is included in the contract that the landlord shall furnish the tenant supplies which may include food, clothes, feed for stock, money or any other thing of value. These advances are to be used only in making the crop. Without such help the tenant would not be able to put in a crop as he is, in most cases, completely without funds. The planters usually have "commissary stores" which furnish these supplies at whatever prices the owners see fit to charge. The tenant has no credit elsewhere and would be forbidden to trade there if he had.* He usually is not permitted to have a vegetable garden because the planter, or a merchant in collusion with the planter, wants to sell as much as possible to the tenant to keep him in debt. The tenant has no recourse. At the time he makes his purchases, he is refused an itemized bill of the articles purchased and the commissary-keeper enters on the books his own figures. Matters go on thus during the work season. When the crop is harvested and sold, and settlement time comes, the tenant gets a slip, simply stating "balance due."[2]

Many workers in turpentine, lumber, and various other kinds of labor camps in the South are defrauded and held in debt in much the same manner as the tenant farmer. One of the customary ways of recruiting workers for these camps

* How well tenants are fed can be seen in figures on deaths from pellagra, a starvation disease. In North Carolina in 1929, according to the State Health Department, there were 981 deaths from this disease.

is for an employer to go to some large center where unemployed workers are seeking jobs. He promises them good wages and conditions. After arriving on the job, the workers find that they are in debt for transportation. Then they go still deeper into debt for food, clothes and additional supplies. In some states they are legally bound to pay off their debts before leaving the job; in others they are held by physical force and terrorism.*

Contrary to popular belief, peonage exists not only in the South, but in the North also. Thus on August 12, 1932, the *Newark* (N. J.) *News* reported that "the padrone system of handling farm labor is flourishing again this summer in five agricultural counties of South Jersey." The report then explains the "padrone" system as follows:

The padrone system is a type of peonage by which farm hands—men, women and children, mostly of Italian extraction—are virtually enslaved to an employment agent. The agent finds work for them, hauls them to the fields, feeds them, sells them merchandise from his store and so indebts them to him that when he collects their wages from the farmer-employer he usually has to return little or nothing to the laborers . . . the padrone system . . . is said to be worse this year because of unemployment than ever before. Farmers employing large numbers of laborers find it a convenient system because it saves them annoyance in handling this type of labor. Employment agents, or padrones, become prosperous under the system. The sufferers are farm hands, who lose their freedom gradually and fall under a mental or actual compulsion.

In the fact that a peon is bound to pay off his debt before he can leave his employer we find the latter's motive in keeping his employee deeply in debt. For the employer is not interested in collecting the debt; he wants to hold the employee in bondage by means of it. By falsifying the accounts,—the employer keeps all the records of debts, pay-

---

* Some of these "free contracts" contain provisions that the laborer consents to allow himself to be locked up in a stockade at night and "at any other time when the employer sees fit to do this." Carter G. Woodson, *The Rural Negro*, pp. 72-73.

ments, contracts—by charging exorbitant interest rates, and by similar practices he keeps the employee perpetually in debt.

Interest rates charged to southern tenant farmers are equivalent to outright robbery. Arthur M. Hyde, Secretary of Agriculture, estimates that the tenant pays 25% on store credit and 35% on fertilizer debts. But even this high estimate is very conservative compared with that made by the North Carolina College of Agriculture after a study of Pitt County farms in 1928. Its figures show that interest rates ranged from 19.1% for cash advances to 72.1% for supplies advanced by merchants.

A peon thus held in debt slavery dares not attempt to leave his employment. If he is foolhardy enough to escape, a man-hunt is organized. Even the "law" takes an active part in these modern hunts for runaway slaves. Sheriffs have frequently been known to cross state lines in order to bring back escaped peons. And when the peons try to leave in large numbers they are held by mass terrorism. For instance, during and after the World War, there was a considerable migration of Negroes from the South to the North. In their efforts to stop it, planters and businessmen's posses halted trains and dragged Negroes from them, dispersed crowds of Negroes waiting for trains to take them North, lynched the discontented, and arrested, mobbed, and fined labor agents who dared hire the Negroes.

Several factors aid the employers in keeping workers or tenant farmers in peonage. Usually the tenant or Negro worker in the peonage sections of the country is unlettered and untraveled, and knows nothing about the outside world. Naturally it is hard for him to break with the old life. And even if the tenant or worker does know of a better place, what can he do? He has no money, no clothes, no means of transportation. He is not skilled and is by no means sure of getting any kind of work elsewhere.

Some of the farm contracts specify, too, that if the cropper or renter fails to perform his contract in every detail he loses not only his crop but all his personal property which, little as it is, may include house furnishings and personal effects. A typical contract of this sort reads in part:

Said tenant further agrees that if he . . . neglects, or abandons, or fails (or in the landlord's judgment violates this contract or fails) to properly work the land early or at proper times, or in case he should become physically incapacitated from working said lands or should die during the term of this lease, or fails to gather the crops when made, or fails to pay the rents or advances made by the owner when due, in which event . . . all indebtedness of the tenant shall at once become due and payable to the owner . . . in which event the owner is hereby authorized to transfer, sell or dispose of all the property thereon the tenant has any interest in. . . .[3]

Naturally the tenant prefers to stick it out in the hope of salvaging something, even if his very life is endangered. Indeed, planters have been known deliberately to force tenants to move after the crop is made and laid by. Thus the planter gets the entire crop and does not have to feed the tenant through the dull months. Under such circumstances the tenant gets nothing for his year's work. However, this happens only when the labor supply is plentiful. Usually the planter is more interested in keeping the peon on the land and employs every means to this end.

As a last resort in holding an adequate supply of labor the planter may keep the tenant's children or wife as hostages.[4] Or he may frame up fake court charges in order to intimidate the serf. Such charges as "rape," "swearing before a female," "shooting across a public road," "vagrancy," and "theft" are among those commonly used.[5]

A county judge in Florida recently told an investigator, "don't you know there's lots of ways of holding niggers? Listen, and I'll tell you how it is done. A boss hires a nigger and gives him a pint of whisky to celebrate. A guard goes around and arrests him for having whisky. The boss tells the nigger he'll bail him out of it, but if the nigger runs away the boss'll let the law jail him for having whisky!" [6]

Then there is the gentlemen's agreement among the planters not to hire each other's croppers, especially if the croppers are in debt as they usually are. In this way an effective blacklist is maintained and the tenant becomes even more entangled in the web which holds him in slavery. But if, in spite of these legal restrictions and practices, any one should try to take laborers or tenants from a planter or employer of any sort, he would be mobbed or shot. A typical case of this sort was reported in the press in 1929. The trouble started when J. T. Wilson, white manager of the Wirewood plantation near Greenwood, Mississippi, went to Macon in that state, signed up 23 families and chartered two freight cars to move them. "When local business men and planters found out what was going on" a large posse was formed and Wilson was given 10 minutes to leave the county—without "his" families. [7]

The fact that the life of a peon is hazardous and any attempt to escape fraught with danger has been admitted by official government publications. An investigator for the U. S. Department of Labor said:

According to the law of the state [Mississippi], only the landlord can give a clear title to the cotton sold. This gives rise to the frequently deferred settlements of which the colored people complain bitterly. Apparently, in order to secure his labor, the landlord often will not settle for the year's work till late in the spring when the next crop has been "pitched." The Negro is then bound hand and foot and must accept the landlord's terms. It usually means that it is impossible for him to get out of the landlord's clutches, no matter how he is being treated. In many cases the Negro does not dare ask for a settlement. Planters often regard it an insult to be required, even by the courts, "to go to their books." A lawyer and planter cited to me the planters' typical excuse: "It is unnecessary to make a settlement, when the tenant is in debt." As to the facts in the case the landlord's word must suffice. . . . The beating of farm hands on the large plantations in the lower

South is so common that many colored people look upon every great plantation as a peon camp; and in sawmills and other public works it is not at all unusual for bosses to knock Negroes around with pieces of lumber or anything else that happens to come handy.[8]

PEONAGE IS LEGALIZED

Apologists for capitalism will admit that peonage existed in the past and that it may still have some hold at present. But they usually say that this is true in spite of laws; that the law is not being enforced. The fact is, on the contrary, that peonage is legalized in several states through the operation of three kinds of laws—vagrancy, emigrant agency, and laws penalizing failure on the part of a tenant farmer or industrial worker to perform a contract after having received advances.

Vagrancy laws are used to secure forced labor especially in the southern states. Any person without work and without visible means of support is a vagrant at the discretion of the judge. The laws are used only against the poorest tenant farmers and industrial workers as well as labor organizers. South Carolina's vagrancy law goes out of its way specifically to include tenants by saying that it also applies to "persons who occupy or being in possession of some piece of land, shall not cultivate enough of it as shall be deemed by the trial justice to be necessary for the maintenance of himself and his family." In Arkansas any person above 14 years of age without work may be arrested for vagrancy under certain circumstances. Vagrancy laws are on the statute books of nearly every state, but they have been used especially in the South.

Carter G. Woodson has given the history of these vagrancy laws. He says:

Immediately after the emancipation of the Negroes in 1865 the devastated States hoped to secure labor by vagrancy laws which compelled every freedman to enter the service of some one and to remain therein for such wages as the ruling classes agreed among themselves to pay. Those freedmen who continued to loiter thereafter were arrested, condemned and put to work on the public highways or leased to planters.

That the law is still being put to its intended use is evidenced by the fact that at present, in order to escape imprisonment as vagrants, tenants and laborers are forced to accept work under any conditions. For example, the *Associated Press* carried a dispatch from Macon, Georgia, August 23, 1930, which read:

Macon police were continuing Saturday their efforts as a volunteer employment bureau for middle Georgia growers. J. H. Stroud of Alma appealed to Chief-of-Police Ben T. Watkins for 50 to 60 unemployed to serve as cotton pickers. Stroud was here Saturday to take the pickers back with him. . . . The city police are rounding up loiterers and offering them jobs or the view of the passing throngs from the inside of the jail. [The charge under such arrests would have been vagrancy.—*W. W.*]

Another and more recent example is contained in the following news item from the New York *Times,* September 26, 1931:

LITTLE ROCK, ARK.—Police action to force unemployed men to help pick this year's bounteous cotton crop to-day had extended from Helena, in Eastern Arkansas, to Bowie County, Texas, on the southwestern border.

Helena and Phillips County officers already have started a drive to get cotton pickers to the fields by threats of vagrancy charges and Bowie County officials to-day said a similar campaign would start there next Monday.

Cotton planters in various sections of the State have complained that they were unable to obtain an adequate number of pickers, despite an unusually large number of unemployed persons.

They attributed the situation to the prevailing low rate of 30 to 40 cents per hundred pounds being paid to pickers, but said a higher price could not be paid because of the low price of cotton.

Helena was free of loiterers to-day, although many Negroes had gone outside the city limits to escape the officers.

Several truckloads of Negroes were captured and sent out to the cotton fields. The sheriff and other officers followed to see that none escaped.

The following news story from Louisiana in 1930 will make it clear why unemployed have to be hunted down and put under guard to work:

At a meeting of 50 leading planters of Caddo and Bossier parishes at the call of Jack P. Fullilove, chairman of the agricultural committee of the Shreveport Chamber of Commerce, it was decided that 50 cents a hundred pounds will be the standard price to be paid cotton pickers in the two parishes this fall.[9]

Since 1930, when this action was taken, as the above story on Arkansas shows, the price for cotton picking has come down to 30 and 40 cents per hundred pounds. Only a few years ago $2 per hundred was being paid. Two hundred pounds of cotton a day is a high average. So the picker who gets the rate of 30 cents a hundred makes 60 cents a day. And then he has to run the risk of never being able to collect even that small amount.

When one of these workers—"bad niggers" and "vagrants"—refuses to toil 10 or 12 hours for 60 cents a day or less and is brought before a judge for his crime, he hasn't a ghost of a chance of being acquitted. The sheriff and court officials in many states are paid by the notorious fee system—so much for each arrest and conviction. Eloquent testimony as to the industry of such officers is contained in their salary figures. In 1929 the sheriff of Bolivar County, Mississippi, received $24,350.70, while the sheriff of Harrison County received $20,401.60 the same year. Other sheriffs averaged around $20,000 a year.[10]

There are other uses for the vagrancy law. Frequently county road building jobs, or even private business men such as planters or turpentine camp operators, need a few hands. Whoever has charge of the work looks around the neighborhood and selects some men—almost always Negroes—whom he would like to have work for him. Then he swears out a warrant for them. The warrant, of course, is based on a vagrancy charge. A typical one was used in Gilchrist County, Florida, in 1930. It specifically names six persons all of whom are in equal degree "rogues, vagabonds, idle or dissolute persons, people who use unlawful games or plays, common pipers and fiddlers . . . persons who neglect their calling (*sic*), or are without reasonable continuous employment, or regular income and who have not sufficient property to sustain them . . . contrary to the statute of this state." On the basis of such a warrant the sheriff obligingly arrests them.

Once convicted on charges of this kind, the newly-made convict is ordered to pay a heavy fine and court costs—which the court promptly pockets under the fee system. At this point the employer who needs the workers generously volunteers to pay the fines and costs provided the victim will sign or touch his pen to a contract agreeing to work out the amount on his plantation or other job.

Emigrant Agency Law

Another law that is a direct aid to peonage practices is the "emigrant agency" law. Such laws are on the statute books of nearly every southern state. They curtail operations of agents who would ship the tenants and laborers to other sections of the South and to the North. Georgia's law is typical of this sort of legislation and reads:

If any person shall, by offering higher wages or in any other way entice, persuade, or decoy, or attempt to entice, persuade, or decoy any servant, cropper or farm laborer, whether under a written or parol contract, after he shall have actually entered the service of his employer, to leave his employer during the term of service, knowing that said servant, cropper, or farm laborer was so employed, he shall be guilty of a misdemeanor.[11]

Texas, which also has its emigrant agency law, passed an auxiliary law in 1930 which forbade any one moving or helping to move the household furnishings and other property of a worker or tenant after nightfall. The effect of such a law, of course, was to prevent peons from escaping during the night.

"Jumping Contract" Law

The favorite legal device used by the southern ruling class to maintain a supply of forced labor is the law which makes it a criminal offense for a laborer or tenant to accept "advances" as part of a contract and then fail—for any reason—to perform that contract to the employer's satisfaction. Such laws are often referred to as "peonage laws," "contract jumping" laws or "false pretense" laws.

The significance of laws of this kind, on the books of several states in 1932, cannot be measured by the number of times workers or tenants are prosecuted under them. It must be measured by the effect they have as swords hanging over the heads of the possible victims. For the worker or tenant who makes a contract and accepts—as he must, being entirely penniless—a loan or supplies of any sort, and then fails for any reason and for any provocation to fulfill that contract, is a "criminal" and is bound for the chain gang at the pleasure of his employer.

The Georgia law, penalizing the breaking of a contract by a worker or tenant, was passed in 1903 after years of experimenting by planters and turpentine bosses in order to get a law that would secure them a supply of forced labor. The law reads in part:

If any person shall contract with another to perform for him services of any kind, with intent to procure money or other thing of value thereby, and not to perform the service contracted for; to the loss and damage of the hirer, or after having so contracted, shall procure from the hirer money, or other thing of value with intent not to perform such service, to the loss and damage of the hirer, he shall be deemed a common cheat and swindler, and upon conviction shall be punished as for a misdemeanor.[12]

Another section was soon added which defined the rules of evidence as to "intent to defraud":

Satisfactory proof of the contract, the procuring thereon of money or other thing of value, the failure to perform the services so contracted for, or failure to return the money so advanced with interest thereon at the time said labor was to be performed, without good and sufficient cause, and loss or damage to the hirer, shall be deemed presumptive evidence of the intent referred to in the preceding section.[13]

Armed with this statute, and controlling the courts and law enforcement machinery generally, from justice-of-the-peace to United States Senator, the planters and other employers obviously have the tenant or laborer at their mercy. Of what value is the "without good and sufficient cause" provision of the above when the planter practically decides what is good cause and what is not?*

This law legalizing peonage was held constitutional by the Georgia State Supreme Court in 1912. The Georgia law has never been tested in the United States Supreme Court.

However, in 1911 an Alabama law, worded almost exactly like the Georgia peonage law cited above, was held unconstitutional in the famous case of Bailey v. State of Alabama.[14] It was found that, as was intended, every case reported under the Alabama statute involved Negro tenants and laborers. The United States Supreme Court in its decision said of the Alabama law that "although the statute in terms is to punish fraud, still its natural and inevitable effect is to expose to conviction for crime those who simply fail or refuse to perform contracts for personal service in liquidation of a debt, and judging its purpose by its effect that it seeks in this way to provide the means of compulsion through which performance of such service may be secured."

* Because of fear of violent retribution, the peonage victim naturally hesitates to testify against a planter. "Investigation has proven that of the hundreds of Negroes lynched in the South during the past half century, a large number died because of their objection to this vicious practice of debt slavery." (See pamphlet, *Black Justice*, published by the American Civil Liberties Union.)

In short the Supreme Court found that the law legalized involuntary servitude. Yet the Georgia law, almost identical, was found to be constitutional by the Georgia Supreme Court in 1912, one year after the decision of the United States Supreme Court in the Bailey *v.* Alabama case.

Compare the text of the Georgia law cited above with the Alabama statute which follows:

Any person, who with intent to injure or defraud his employer, enters into a contract in writing for the performance of any act of service, and thereby obtains money or other personal property from such employer, and with like intent, and without just cause, and without refunding such money, or paying for such property, refuses or fails to perform such act or service, must on conviction be punished by a fine in double the damage suffered by the injured party, but not more than $300, one-half of said fine to go to the county and one-half to the party injured; and any person, who with intent to injure or defraud his landlord, enters into any contract in writing for the rent of land, and thereby obtains any money or other personal property from such landlord, and with like intent, without just cause, and without refunding such money, or paying for such property, refuses or fails to cultivate such land, or to comply with his contract relative thereto, must on conviction be punished by fine in double the damage suffered by the injured party, but not more than $300, one-half of said fine to go to the county and one-half to the party injured. And the refusal or failure of any person, who enters into such contract, to perform such act or service or to cultivate such land, or refund such money, or pay for such property without just cause shall be prima facie evidence of the intent to injure his employer or landlord or defraud him. That all laws and parts of laws in conflict with the provisions hereof be and the same are hereby repealed.[15]

Now compare both the Alabama and Georgia laws with one passed in Florida as late as 1919, or eight years after the Alabama law, as cited above, was declared unconstitutional by the United States Supreme Court. No essential difference can be seen in the provisions of the three. The Florida law follows:

Any person in this state who shall, with intent to injure and defraud, under and by reason of a contract or promise to perform labor or service, procure or obtain money or other thing of value as a credit, or as advances, shall be guilty of a misdemeanor and upon conviction thereof shall be punished by a fine not exceeding $500 or by imprisonment not exceeding six months.

In all prosecutions for a violation of this section the failure or refusal, without just cause, to perform such labor or service or to pay for the money or other thing of value so obtained or procured shall be prima facie evidence of the intent to injure and defraud.[16]

The Florida law was passed under the Governorship of Sidney J. Catts, who in his campaign speeches promised "to put the niggers in their places." Catts was tried in Federal court on peonage charges soon after his term of office expired but because of his influence was acquitted. The interests back of the law, according to Orland K. Armstrong, former head of the Department of Journalism at the University of Florida, who made an investigation of the law and interviewed members of the 1919 legislature that passed it, were the turpentine and lumber interests of the state. Armstrong visited turpentine camps operated by convict labor where there were many "contract jumpers" (persons convicted of violating this law). Armstrong says, "It is safe to assume that most of these men sentenced to the gang on the basis of the 1919 law were recruited under misrepresentation; were forced to work under intolerable conditions; were caught and held under warrants that assert a misdemeanor under an unconstitutional law, and sentenced without a semblance of a defense for fraud." [17]

The story is told of how a white planter in a county in Georgia had a young Negro arrested for failing to comply with his contract. The young man had been drafted into the United States Army during the World War. He pleaded that that was the reason he was forced to break the contract. But that was not "a good and sufficient cause," so he was held. A Negro farmer was in the act of signing the young man's bond, when the white planter flew into a rage, saying "No nigger shall help another nigger to beat me out of my money," and shot the farmer.[18]

Several other states have laws, similar to those quoted above, which legalize peonage.* But, of course, when the ruling class of a section endorses peonage it makes very little difference what the law permits. The ruling class will do what is to its advantage. Senator Walter F. George, of Georgia, for five years a member of the Georgia Supreme Court, openly admitted this when he wrote in *Liberty,* April 21, 1928:

No statutory law, no organic law, no military law supersedes the law of social necessity and social identity.

Why apologize or evade? We have been very careful to obey the letter of the Federal Constitution—but we have been very diligent in violating the spirit of such amendments and such statutes as would have a Negro to believe himself the equal of a white man. And we shall continue to conduct ourselves in that way.

---

* There is another important legal practice in the South which has a bearing on peonage, and that is "legal lynching." Many of the "executions" of Negroes are only subtle lynchings aimed to avoid adverse criticism which would follow the crude rope and faggot method. In the year ending July 1, 1931, 68 Negroes were "legally" executed in the southern states. A typical example of how everything is made ready for a legal lynching is seen in the famous Scottsboro, Alabama, case.

CHAPTER VII

PEONAGE EXPOSED

SOME idea of the seriousness of the peonage problem in this country can be gained by reviewing a few of the actual prosecutions since 1903. For, despite precautions taken by the planters and the inactivity of the Department of Justice, which has jurisdiction over such cases, and in spite of terrorism, stories leak out and prosecutions are forced. The total number of such prosecutions and complaints cannot be learned, as in recent years the Department of Justice has refused to make public its report on this phase of its work. But even if an annual report of prosecutions and reported cases were available it would not tell the smallest part of the whole story, for obviously only a very few of the total number of cases are prosecuted or even reported.

In 1903 the Federal Grand Jury at Montgomery, Alabama, returned about 100 indictments for peonage.[1] In 1907 there were 83 peonage complaints pending in the Department of Justice.

At that time many white families and individuals were enmeshed in this system of forced labor.* *Collier's* magazine, July 24, 1909, tells the story of Joseph Callas, a Russian Jew, who was arrested in Little Rock, Arkansas, while *en route* to California in search of work. He was taken to a prison in southeast Arkansas where 145 Negroes and whites were held. A sub-contractor in 1907 hired 60 Poles and paid

* Contract labor is here classed under peonage. This form of forced labor arose toward the close of the Civil War with the organization of the American Immigrant Co. which brought immigrants to the United States under contract to work a certain number of years. To enforce the contract the immigrant's wages could be legally pledged; also there were laws penalizing breaking of such a contract.[2] *Encyclopædia of the Social Sciences,* Vol. 4, pp. 342-44.

their fare from New York to Greenville, N. C., where they were put to work on the Norfolk and Southern Railroad. They soon saw what they were up against and quit, whereupon a local justice of the peace issued warrants for their arrest for "obtaining goods under false pretenses."

The situation in this country regarding immigrants became so serious that the Italian government, after seeing its nationals enslaved and slain in Louisiana, warned natives of Italy to stay away from the South. Austria and Hungary in like manner blacklisted Mississippi and Missouri.[2]

The publicity that arose from such protests and exposures caused Congress, in 1908, to request the Immigration Commission to "investigate" immigrants' conditions on cotton plantations, turpentine farms, lumber and railway camps. The resolution as first introduced applied only to the South, but the outraged southern ruling class insisted that what was going on in the North and West was just as bad as in the South. As a result of these counter charges the scope of the resolution was broadened to include the entire country.

The subcommittee on peonage appointed by the Immigration Commission stated that "peonage cases in the South relating to immigrants have been found to cover almost every industry—farming, lumbering, logging, railroading, mining, factories and construction work."

But it was of Maine in the North, that the investigating committee of 1908 said: "There has probably existed in Maine the most complete system of peonage in the entire country." In 1907 a law was passed in this state which made it a crime for a laborer who had received "advances" to leave the employment before he has worked long enough to repay the employer. The investigating committee, after an examination of conditions in the logging and lumbering industries, reported, "Considerable peonage has resulted from the statute. . . . Involuntary servitude results in utilizing this statute to intimidate laborers to work against their will. . . .

If a man leaves his employer before settling for advances, he will be pursued and apprehended."

The committee also found something close to peonage in the padrone system in shoe-shining establishments reported from many parts of the West. Also "in some of the lumber and railroad camps in Minnesota and North Dakota laborers were held in a state of technical peonage." It gives little exact information but broadly, it says, "undoubted evidence has been discovered that peonage has been practiced in the western states, and the indications are that there are many cases of involuntary servitude in that section." Summing up, the committee says that, "in every state except Oklahoma and Connecticut the investigator found evidences of practices between employer and employee which, if substituted by legal evidence in each case, would constitute peonage as the Supreme Court has described it." [8]

Cases of this type can still be found—and outside the South. For example, the Buffalo *Evening News* recently won a prize for meritorious news reporting when it exposed peonage in northern New York in August and October, 1931. It existed at the labor camps operated by construction companies on the Sardinia-Springville state road project and in the building of the new Attica prison. Workers were required to live in cowbarns in which as many as 96 double deck cots had been jammed. Commissary charges were deducted from their meager wages, though a state law forbids such deductions. Whisky was sold and the price deducted from wages. If a worker bought no whisky, he was charged for it just the same. A large number of men found to their surprise that they had no pay coming to them. Eight dollars a week was charged for sleeping room in the barn. Then acting Governor Lehman was "aroused by reports that laborers on state construction jobs lived like peons and were treated like coolies" and finally ordered state officers to "investigate."

In 1920 widespread peonage was reported in Early, Dooly,

Worth, Decatur, Toombs and Morgan counties, Georgia.[4]
Governor Hugh M. Dorsey of Georgia followed this in 1921
with his report on *The Negro in Georgia* in which he listed
almost two dozen known cases of peonage in its worst form.
Shortly after the Dorsey report the notorious John S.
Williams "murder farm" cases were exposed. It was found
that on this single farm at least 11 croppers were killed
because "they knew too much" or because it became certain
that the Department of Justice would be forced to investigate.

There were many cases prosecuted in 1925. Two of the
best known were those of four men from Anderson County,
South Carolina, who were sentenced to Federal imprisonment
at Atlanta. M. B. Davis and Charles Land, turpentine
operators of Calhoun County, Florida, along with three other
men, were also convicted of peonage by a Federal jury
in 1925.[5]

In Corpus Christi and Raymondville, Texas, four white
men (the sheriff, two deputies and a justice-of-the-peace)
were found guilty of peonage practices. Four young white
boys, all under 21 years of age, one of them a former page
in the National House of Representatives, went to a cotton
picking job where they had been promised pay of $1.25 per
hundred pounds and free board. On the job they found that
they were being forced to pay board. They became dis-
satisfied and left and were arrested in Raymondville on
"vagrancy" charges and given the alternative of working for
their original employer or being prosecuted and sent to the
chain gang.[6]

In 1927 some big cases were exposed in Amite County,
Mississippi. Two wealthy planters of this county went into
Louisiana for escaped Negroes and brought them back to
Mississippi. In this same county Webb Bellue and John D.
Alford, prominent citizens, were convicted of selling Craw-
ford Allen, fifty-year-old Negro, his wife and three children
for $20.[7] Bellue and Alford seized Allen and his family for

a debt of $20 and transported them to a farm near Fluker, Louisiana, where they were forced to work several weeks without pay. Afterwards they were sold. A short time later W. D. Arnold, a middle Georgia planter, was indicted on peonage charges for holding a white man, Claude King, and a Negro, John Vanover.

CATASTROPHES EXPOSE PEONAGE

A big "act of God" is a better investigator of peonage, apparently, than the Department of Justice, for such catastrophes usually bring to light peonage cases by the wholesale. In 1927, for example, the Mississippi River flooded a vast territory including much of the peonage country. Several hundred thousand white and black tenants and laborers were thrown on the doles of that "Wonderful Mother," the Red Cross. It is a matter of record that the planters at first refused to let their tenants be removed from the plantations for fear they might escape. Then when the waters began to enter the cabins a deal was made between the Red Cross and the planters by which the Red Cross agreed to have the National Guard stand guard over the tenants, and when the waters subsided, to deliver them, even against their will, back to the plantations whence they came.[8]

In the encampments the croppers, renters, and laborers were closely watched by guardsmen. No one could leave the camp without a permit. Several of the flood victims were shot, some while trying to escape. Still, many escaped. Thousands were conscripted into levee building and work for private employers on other jobs without pay. When the floods receded, the Red Cross, the National Guard, and the overseers from various plantations staged a "round-up" of the reluctant victims, herded them into barges and returned them to their masters. During the flood, the Arizona Cotton Growers' Association applied to the Federal Employment offices for 4,000 workers from among the refugees, offering them about four months' work. But, according to the general

manager of this Association, the employment offices refused
to negotiate the deal because "any move of this nature would
be fought by the different users of this class of labor throughout the districts affected." [9]

Even after the flood the doles had to be continued. The
Red Cross policy of local autonomy for branches in giving
out relief gave the planters, of course, a chance to have their
own representatives at the head of relief distribution. In
order to facilitate the distribution many planters "generously"
offered the use of their plantation commissaries as store-
houses for the food and other supplies. Then the same goods
were sold or given away at the planter's discretion and to his
personal advancement.[10]

In 1930 came another "act of God." This time God dried
up the same country he had flooded in 1927. One of the
worst famines in the country's entire history followed a pro-
longed drought in the southern states bordering the Mississippi River. Widespread peonage was uncovered. Reports
came out of the drought country that terrible conditions
existed especially in Louisiana and Arkansas. More specific
locations were given around Bald Knob and Searcy, Arkansas,
as well as in St. Francis County. A professor in one of the
schools in Conway, Arkansas, told Russell Owen, correspondent of the New York *Times,* that "Some of the farmers
... had been in debt so many years that they no longer sought
a statement of their accounts. They were in bondage so deep
they did not care." [11]

The *Times* reported that the "share-cropper made nothing
last year. He owes the planter for his food and clothing and
must hope to work it out. The share-cropper can't move to
another plantation unless his debts are assumed by the new
planter." It was found in other sections of the drought
country, as well as in Arkansas, that the Negro croppers were
living as well on the doles—an average of $3\frac{1}{2}$ cents per
meal per person [12]—as under normal conditions, and that the
planters had to bargain with the Red Cross to restrict the

doles in order to keep the croppers satisfied on the plantations.   Owen reported much grumbling about the "Red
Cross freeing the Negro."

How the Red Cross freed the Negroes is well illustrated
by an *Associated Press* dispatch from Yazoo City, Mississippi:

In order to keep laborers from deserting farms in Yazoo
County, the county Red Cross Chapter has cut down on drought
relief and now is administering only to cases of extreme destitu-
tion. Planters requested discontinuance of the daily distributions,
saying hundreds of laborers were leaving farms. . . .[13]

In other places the Red Cross was reported to have told
tenants "if you leave the crop, relief will be cut off."   In
other words, acceptance of their status as forced laborers was
the condition for receiving relief.

But these cases of wholesale exposure can happen only
infrequently. Less spectacular cases, however, continually
crop out in the press. Every week cases of shooting affairs
between landlord and tenant are reported. On the surface
there is little significance in such happenings, but closer
analysis reveals that most of them occur over divisions of the
crop and as a result of peonage. The writer has hundreds of
newspaper clippings dealing with such cases, including many
in which white tenants are involved.

OTHER RECENT PEONAGE CASES

Some recent and direct cases of peonage can be cited to
prove that no later than a few months ago, this system of
forced labor was being practiced in many sections of the
country.

In 1928 Thelma Duncan, a North Carolina school teacher,
reported cases of peonage in that state.[14]   In 1929, Orland
K. Armstrong, university of Florida professor, made a damn-
ing exposé of peonage laws and practices in Florida. He
cited many cases of Negroes being sold to turpentine companies at from $50 to $150 each. He was surprised to find

very few prosecutions and convictions, and asked lawyers, legislators and business men for the reason. A typical reply was given by a business man:

Do you want to know why they can't get any convictions? Here's why—suppose they arrest some operators. All right. Now bring them into court. They are men of wealth and respectability. They own big property. They elect the county and state officers. Who's the jury? Men who owe 'em money! Accuse 'em of peonage. They bring in records to show they don't owe a Negro a penny. The owner, the boss men, the bookkeeper, the commissary clerk all testify. And what else? Every big company has favorite Negroes, who get good wages and act as straw bosses. They put them on the stand. They've been working for that company for years; paid every month and never mistreated. And against that line-up, you got a poor devil of an ignorant nigger off a chain gang! Think you can convict? [15]

In March, 1930, James E. Piggott, prominent Washington Parish, Louisiana, planter, pleaded guilty of holding Negro farm workers in peonage. Piggott told Federal Judge Borah that "I handled Negroes in the same way every one else in the South does." He admitted that on several occasions his croppers escaped into Mississippi and that Louisiana officers went after them and brought them back without any sort of requisition papers or warrants.[16]

Another typical case in Louisiana occurred in 1931. J. M. McLemore of Coushatta was charged with peonage practices. The investigation disclosed that McLemore habitually carried a pistol with which to shoot any one attempting to escape.

PEONAGE ON GOVERNMENT JOB

One of the most recent exposés of peonage involved work done for the United States government. In December, 1931, it was discovered that the War Department was using compulsory labor on levee work under its supervision along the Mississippi River. Gross brutality was charged including the flogging and beating of Negro workers with leather straps,

clubs and pistol butts, for not doing enough work or for
minor infraction of camp rules.   Men were forced to work
12 to 18 hours a day.   The pay rate was from 75 cents to
$2 a day for skilled labor.   For unskilled it was much less.
Trading in the commissary was compulsory and charges for
"stuff" were exorbitant.   There was an arbitrary deduction
of $4.50 a week from each man's pay for commissary sup-
plies, whether the supplies were purchased or not.   Thirty
contractors with offices in New Orleans, St. Louis, Kansas
City, Cleveland and Pittsburgh were declared to be involved.
Meanwhile the War Department has ordered an "investigation." [17]

   This record of peonage prosecutions and exposés bears out
the results of a peonage questionnaire recently sent by the
author to about 150 prominent teachers, lawyers, state officials and other professional people in every part of the South.
The majority of replies showed that peonage does exist in
these states.   A former member of the Texas Senate said,
"the system of binding tenant-croppers to the soil does not
exist in Texas in theory.   It is recognized by force, has a
firm hold and terrorizes the tenant."   A former deputy labor
commissioner of Texas also admitted that "Peonage actually
exists in this state."   Replies from other states were similar.
The editor of a Louisiana weekly said, "in the sugar districts
the condition of labor is that of out-and-out peonage, and it is
the same in the lumber industry."   Officials in the department
of charities and public welfare in several states said peonage
existed to some extent.   *In almost every case those who
replied to this questionnaire asked that their names should
not be published.*
   Peonage is not a thing of the past.   It exists now in many
sections of the United States.   It is legal in several states
and is practiced in others, though "illegal."   There is evidence that since the beginning of the present economic crisis,
employers in the peonage country, in order to secure lower

labor costs, have increased their exploitation. At the same time an increasing number of small farmers are losing their small holdings and entering the ranks of the tenant. According to the last census over 60% of all southern farmers are tenants.

REBELLION AND STRUGGLE

The workers and tenants held in peonage have waged many militant battles against these conditions. In many of these struggles Negroes and whites fought shoulder to shoulder. The landlords and other employers, with the help of the law and the courts, have drowned in blood most of the attempts at organization.

No adequate study of organization and struggle among workers and tenant peons has ever been made. The records on the subject are poor and scattered and no attempt has been made to gather even these. However, a brief summary of some of the most important struggles can be given here.

In Sandersville, Georgia, in 1884, it was reported that a man had arrived from Louisville, Kentucky, for the purpose of organizing Negro tenants and farm workers into unions to get higher wages and better conditions. The report concluded typically enough with this sentence: "The militia have been sent for."

The experiences of Hiram F. Hoover who came to middle Georgia from Hickory, North Carolina, in 1887 to organize the share croppers show that organizers at that time were treated just as harshly as to-day. At Warrenton, Georgia, he was shot by a posse of planters and left for dead. Although half his face was blown away, he survived. When it was learned that he still lived, an Augusta paper said, "The general verdict here is that they should have killed him." Hoover continued in his "crimes" of organizing the Negroes and moved to Madison where he was told by the best (wealthiest) citizens to leave. It was reported that while he was recovering from his wounds his wife continued his work

—so a committee "waited on her." He tried to work in several other places but was continually hounded and persecuted. Finally he was driven out of the South.

One of the most important of the early efforts to organize southern tenant farmers on a large scale was the attempt in 1891 to form a Colored Farmers Alliance of the United States. Its headquarters were in Houston, Texas. A cotton pickers' strike was called for September 12, 1891. Southern newspapers became alarmed over the "threat." The official Farmers Alliance (white), dominated by wealthy farmers and business men, immediately attacked the Negro organization, condemned the strike and helped the planters to defeat it.

One of the more recent and most brutal suppressions of a tenant farmers' union took place at Elaine, Phillips County, Arkansas, in 1919. The Arkansas union was very conservative. The charter was drawn up by Williamson and Williamson, white lawyers. Members of this tenant-farmers' union had to be churchgoers and swear to defend the Constitution of the United States. But the union was militant in wanting to wage a fight on peonage which was particularly vicious in Phillips County. When the union met in a church to lay plans and to retain a lawyer—a white man, who had been a Federal attorney and former postmaster—it was attacked by an armed mob of planters and business men. The church was burned to the ground and the croppers hunted down like wild beasts. It is estimated that close to 200 were slaughtered. The Negroes resisted and though they were poorly armed killed some white attackers.

Hundreds of the croppers were then arrested charged with insurrection, murder and other crimes. Not a single white man was arrested. After a "fair trial" at which the croppers were "defended" by a lawyer appointed by the court, 12 were sentenced to death and 67 to long term imprisonment. The trial lasted three-quarters of an hour. It took a jury of planters or their hirelings seven minutes to condemn 12 men to death. Not a single Negro was on the jury or on the panel; a threatening mob and troops were present; the croppers' lawyer had no preliminary consultation with the defendants; he never called a single witness even though they were available. Shortly after the arrest of the croppers a mob marched to the jail to lynch them but was prevented by the Committee of Seven and other leading citizens and officials who promised if the mob refrained, they would execute those found guilty in the form of law.

Later when appeals were made to the Governor of Arkansas for clemency the American Legion, the Lions Club, and the Helena Rotary Club held meetings, attended by representatives of the leading industrial and commercial enterprises of Helena, passed resolutions asking the Governor to ignore the appeal. The American Legion resolution stated that a "solemn promise was given by the leading citizens of the community that if the guilty parties were not lynched, and let the law take its course, that justice would be done and the majesty of the law upheld." [18] Members of the Legion were very active in the man-hunts in which scores of the croppers were killed. Several members of the Legion were also killed.

Later one of the chief motives of the planters in breaking up the tenants' union was brought out. For "Negro prisoners are said to have confessed, each member of the organization at specified times was to take a bale of cotton . . . to certain prominent landowners, plantation-managers, and merchants and demand a settlement." [19] It will be recalled that the refusal to make settlements is one of the methods of enforcing peonage. The Negro tenants had positive evidence that the planters of Phillips County were preparing to ship off the cotton—in which the croppers theoretically had a share—and to sell it without settling with the tenants or allowing them to sell their share of the crop.

Industrial workers have also struggled against actual peonage. On November 22, 1919, in Bogalusa, Louisiana, three white men were shot dead, and a number severely wounded in such a struggle. The white men were killed because they had dared walk down the main street of Bogalusa, with guns on their hips, protecting with their lives and guns the life of a Negro labor organizer.[20]

The Great Southern Lumber Company which owns Bogalusa had an auxiliary organization called the Loyalty League. It was formed during the war and made up of business men. The chief function of the organization was to see that every able-bodied man—especially Negroes—should work at any task, at any wage and for any hours that the employer might desire. In 1919 the situation was such that a labor leader reported:

They have been continually arresting Negroes for vagrancy and placing them in the city jail. It seems that a raid is made each night in the section of the town where the Negroes live and all that can be found are rounded up and placed in jail charged with vagrancy. In the morning the Great Southern Lumber Company goes to the jail and takes them before the city court where they are fined as vagrants and turned over to the lumber company, under the guard of the gunmen, where they are made to work out this fine. There is one old Negro in the hospital in New Orleans whom they went to see one night, and ordered to be at the mill at work next day. The old man was not able to work, and was also sick at the time. They went back the next night and beat the old man almost to death and broke both of his arms between the wrist and the elbow.[21]

It was out of such conditions that a hard-fought strike arose, in which, as has been mentioned, three white men were killed while protecting a Negro organizer, thus furnishing one of the most important examples of solidarity between white and Negro workers to be found in the history of the United States.

In the summer of 1931, to cite another and even more significant case, white and Negro tenants in and around Camp Hill, Alabama, were organized by the Trade Union Unity League into a militant union. The main purpose of this avowedly militant union is in one respect no different from that of the tenants' union in Arkansas in 1919, namely—to fight peonage. Alabama planters, emulating their ruling class brothers in Arkansas, also attacked a union meeting which was being held in a church near Camp Hill. The church was burned to the ground, one man was murdered on the spot in cold blood and four others were sent to "cut stove wood," a euphemistic term for lynching. Some 35 were rounded up and arrested.

Certain liberal organizations and individuals, including the National Association for the Advancement of Colored People and its officials, William Pickens, Walter White and W. E. B. DuBois, following their usual policy, played into the hands of the lynchers by saying that the Communists were to be blamed for thus disturbing the "good relations" between the tenants and the planters. In reality peonage was responsible, and the Communists must be credited with waging a relentless fight against peonage. Students of the labor movement have long recognized that any attempt of industrial workers to organize in unions to better their economic position will be fought by employers with bullets, clubs, gas and every other weapon available. The same principle obviously holds true with attempts of agricultural workers and tenant farmers to improve their economic position.

The Camp Hill union, in coöperation with the International Labor Defense, was able to win the freedom of all the 35 arrested members. And for the first time in the long history of struggles against peonage, this Camp Hill union was able to beat back the attacks of the employers and win certain demands. As a result it came out of the attack stronger and more solidly entrenched than ever. It has even been able to extend its organization into adjoining counties, organizing a majority of the Negro croppers in many localities.

The demands of the Share Croppers Union at Camp Hill were: (1) continuation of food allowance which had been cut off July 1, after the crop was cultivated and "laid by," leaving the cropper to starve or beg until cotton picking time in

September, (2) right of the cropper to sell his produce for cash where and when he pleased, rather than turn it over to the landlord for "division," (3) cash settlement for the season at cotton picking time, (4) a 9-months' school for Negro children as well as white with free bus, (5) right of the cropper to have his own garden.[22] The two specific demands won were extension of food allowance to November 1 and permission to grow gardens for the use of the tenant.

Notasulga, a few miles from Camp Hill, witnessed a more recent armed attack upon Negro share croppers. On December 19, 1932, the sheriff and a posse came to the home of a Share Croppers Union leader in an attempt to seize his mule at the behest of the landowner. Other croppers came to the defense of their leader to resist the organized terror of the authorities. In the struggle that followed a number of croppers were killed, others were wounded and thirteen Negroes arrested. Two of the union leaders died a few days later from wounds received, after having been turned over to the police by the officials of the Tuskegee Institute to whom they had come for hospital treatment.

PEONAGE AMONG MEXICANS IN THE UNITED STATES

Just as intolerable as the peonage that binds Negroes in the South is the peonage to which Mexicans are subjected in the United States. Though no formal study has been made of the situation it is well recognized that much of the work in the industries in the Southwest—projects in the Lower Rio Grande Valley, the Imperial Valley in southern California, big ranches, railroad construction, irrigation jobs—has been done by Mexican workers slaving under peonage. Thousands of Mexican forced laborers have toiled in the beet fields of Colorado, Kansas and other states.

In at least one instance the United States government has intervened in behalf of the employers in the Southwest in order to enable them to get their talons on forced labor. This action included the Rainey Amendment to the Emergency

Immigration Bill which permitted ranchers, planters and other employers to import a large number of Mexicans. Under this law the employers were to guard the workers so that when they were through with them they could deport them to Mexico. Under the law these workers were not permitted to seek other employment or leave the employment of the man who had imported them.

To create divisions between Mexican and American workers the capitalist sources of information have always been used to build up a myth that Mexican workers are "inferior creatures." But when business men of the Southwest wanted an even larger supply of forced labor, the government obligingly waived all immigration restrictions, including the literacy test and head tax. The workers, however, were not allowed to come as free men but were to be held on the job on which they were imported to work. No matter how intolerable conditions they could not leave it. And when they were no longer needed they were to be deported.

Under the Rainey Amendment the Arizona Cotton Growers Association alone admitted using around 35,000 of these contract laborers. Ranchers under this law also arbitrarily seized Mexicans wherever they could. Most of the Mexican workers did not speak English and were carried into sections where the ranchers dominated the political situation. Obviously under such circumstances the workers were at the mercy of their employers.

It frequently happened that these peons became desperate and tried to escape. Then posses of the masters "arrested" them and brought them back or in some cases deported them under cover of guns. The threat of such "arrests" and deportations always hung over the workers as a penalty for protesting their lot. Long after the war-time emergency had passed the workers were still being held.

Peonage is practiced on the salmon canning fleets of the Pacific Northwest. Helpless, unemployed Mexicans are forced to sign a contract agreeing, on penalty of fines from

$10 to $50 for each "offense," to work on Sundays, holidays or nights when asked to do so by their employers. They also agree that if they quit work because of strikes or any other reason, all their wages will be forfeited.[23] Officials of the United States Bureau of Fisheries made an investigation and verified the charges, and in addition reported that after a laborer had signed a contract and was taken to a canning factory it was virtually impossible for him to escape. About 29,000 Mexican, Filipino, Chinese and Japanese laborers were employed in such canneries in 1929 in Alaska alone.

Texas, like other southern states, has its law restricting employment agencies which would ship Mexican and Negro workers from Texas to other sections of the country. The law was passed as a deliberate measure to keep a monopoly on cheap forced labor. The State Federation of Labor (A. F. of L.) supported this peonage bill!

An officer of the Texas Department of Agriculture recently wrote the author that the state had about 400,000 Mexican farm workers or tenants; that they were paid about half the wages received by native Americans. He described their conditions as a "shame without any question." Then, a little later, an official of the Department of Labor wrote, in reply to a questionnaire on peonage, that one of the worst blots on the state was the peonage practices directed against Mexican workers. He explained, moreover, that very few prosecutions arose because the system "was so plausibly explained" as to dupe both Federal and State authorities. He was very naïve.

The general solicitor of the Sante Fe railroad, E. E. McInnes, recently admitted before a Congressional committee, that over 75% of all their track workers in the Southwest are Mexicans. When asked by Congressman George J. Schneider of Wisconsin, "How do you get this labor?" he replied, "Our workers are furnished by Holmes and Company of Los Angeles and San Francisco without charge." It was brought out that the reason that this employment agency could afford to supply workers free was that it was given the concession to operate commissaries in the railroad camps. They made their profit in that way, charging whatever they chose, falsified the accounts, and held the whip of discharge over the workers through coöperation with the railroad company.

In face of such conditions the American Federation of Labor officialdom has a record of attacking the Mexican workers. It has refused to organize them and even refuses to admit them into unions when their applications for membership are presented. There is a gentlemen's agreement in many unions in the Southwest, including the longshoremen (International Longshoremen's Association), that all Mexican workers shall be "black-balled."

The Mexican cantaloupe pickers in the Imperial Valley, California, went on strike in 1928 for better wages and to end conditions equivalent to peonage. All the forces of "law and order" including the courts and the sheriff helped to crush the strike. Halls were raided and closed without warrant. Bail for arrested workers was set as high as $1,000 on vagrancy charges based on the fact that the workers were on strike and therefore not working. "The purpose was, of course, to prevent organization of the Mexicans. . . ." [24]

The latest strike in the Imperial Valley, in 1930, was led by the Agricultural Workers Industrial Union affiliated to the Trade Union Unity League. The same sheriff who broke the 1928 strike with his forces finally broke this strike. Six organizers were sentenced to from three to 42 years in California's bastilles for their activities. Others were deported to Mexico. This union is organizing workers in the Imperial Valley as well as in the Colorado beet fields where peonage also exists. [25] On May 16, 1932, some 18,000 of these Colorado beet workers went on strike under the leadership of this union. They struck against the intolerable conditions of peonage and lowered rates.

CHAPTER VIII

FORCED LABOR IN THE COLONIES

ALTHOUGH much direct forced labor exists in the homeland of every capitalist country, it prevails to a much greater extent in the colonies. In nearly all colonial and semicolonial countries there are laws, regulations and practices which make it compulsory for the majority of the native population to work for a definite time, directly or indirectly, for foreign capitalists without pay or for only a nominal wage.

How are forced laborers recruited in the colonies? The methods employed for creating forced labor here are similar to those employed by the early capitalists in creating wage laborers. Generally, the first wage laborers were created by forcibly robbing the peasants of their means of livelihood, by driving them from the land and often burning their homes. Cut off from their accustomed means of earning a living they were forced to accept work wherêver and however offered.

In the colonies various methods have been used to take the land away from the natives. It has been expropriated by force, either outright or "legalized" by legislation. The Union of South Africa provides a good example of such land theft. Some five and a half million natives are herded into reservations consisting of some 60,000,000 acres of the worst land, while the 1,500,000 European population (white) occupies 240,000,000 acres of the best land.

One of the shrewdest and most "civilized" methods used by the imperialists in breaking up the agricultural system of the natives and converting the peasants into forced laborers is to impose heavy taxes on them. There are many kinds of such taxes: tax on the harvest; a poll tax which often must be paid in "kind," *i.e.*, by forced labor; taxes which the natives pay in lieu of forced labor; and others. This heavy taxation gradually ruins the natives and compels them to apply to the large capitalist plantations, factories, or mines for work in order to secure money with which to pay taxes. *If they are not paid the natives are jailed and forced to do penal forced labor.*

Among the other methods of securing forced labor is the use of restrictive laws such as vagrancy and pass laws under which persons refusing to work on the terms offered, or persons without credentials, are arrested and sentenced to labor. Besides, native chiefs are often bribed or compelled to supply laborers. Colonial governments, in making concessions to foreign capitalists, often agree to coöperate in securing a plentiful supply of forced labor. Often direct conscription or armed "recruiting" is resorted to by such governments. Such "recruiting" closely resembles the early slave raids.

The types of forced labor in the colonies range from outright chattel slavery to various types of labor on the borderline between forced labor and wage labor. Of the five or six million slaves in the world some two million are in Abyssinia. There are hundreds of thousands of them in Arabia, in the British protectorate of Sierra Leone, in China —it has been estimated that there are two million child slaves in China—and elsewhere.

Of much greater importance is the peonage system which varies in form according to the economic conditions of the particular colonial or semi-colonial country. Peonage is the most widespread type of forced labor in the territories over which the imperialist régime of Wall Street holds its sway. Professor E. A. Ross of the University of Wisconsin declares that from the Rio Grande down the west coast of South America to Cape Horn "the laborers on the estates are at various stages of mitigation of the once universal slavery into which the native population were crushed by the iron heel of the conquistador."

Other types of forced labor used in colonial countries, including those under the heel of American imperialism, are "contract labor"—enforced by law, violence and terrorism—and labor on "public works" for colonial governments, much of which is, in reality, done for private capitalists. There is also the practice of forcing peasants to grow food for the use of forced laborers on certain jobs; and, of course, convict labor which is performed both by native prisoners and often by thousands of political prisoners exiled to the colonies for struggling against capitalism. And vagrancy laws are used even more cruelly than in the imperialist countries. In the Kenya Colony of British East Africa, for example, these laws force "vagrants" and juveniles without parental support, into practical slavery.

PRODUCTS OF FORCED LABOR

The hypocrisy of the United States in its policy with regard to forced labor was clearly illustrated during the discussion on Section 307 of the United States Tariff Act of 1930, which bans the importation into the United States of goods produced wholly or in part by forced labor. This section of the Tariff Act was aimed specifically at Soviet-American trade. However, to avoid any criticism that it was discriminatory legislation much righteous indignation was expressed by the legislators against forced labor in general and the law was at first prepared to apply to all countries alike. In that way, it was felt, the ban on goods from the Soviet Union could be justified.

Then the startling fact was revealed that about one-fifth of the total imports into the United States are products which in whole or in part result from one of the forms of direct forced labor. These include rubber, coffee, sugar, cocoa, tea, tobacco, as well as fruits and nuts in addition to certain oils, spices, minerals and related products. Coffee in Brazil, Guatemala and other countries; rubber in Sumatra, Liberia and elsewhere; fruits in Central America, the land of peonage; tobacco in Sumatra, Cuba and other countries— these are some of the countries and products contributing to the imports of the United States.

Imagine the consternation of the big sugar refining companies, the coffee dealers and roasters; the tire manufacturers—Goodyear, Firestone and others; the United Fruit Co., the Anaconda Copper Co., the Mellon companies, the Rockefeller oil interests and other concerns when they found that the ban might also be applied to their goods. The crusading fervor of the legislators waned. A rider was then obligingly tacked on the Tariff Act providing that goods not produced in the United States in sufficient quantities to satisfy the demand were not to be included in the ban on forced labor products, regardless of how much forced labor was used in their production!

While a considerable part of these forced-labor-tainted goods are produced in colonies of foreign imperialists—those under the rule of England, France, Portugal, the Netherlands, and Belgium, a very large part comes from colonies or semi-colonies of the United States or countries in which a huge amount of American finance capital is invested. In fact, in every one of the colonies, semi-colonies and "independent" countries where American capital is invested, Wall Street imperialism is using forced labor either directly or indirectly. A list of the most "respectable" citizens engaged in this exploitation of colonial forced labor would include some of the biggest capitalists in the United States such as Rockefeller, Guggenheim, Ford, Mellon, Morgan and many others. They super-exploit this labor in much the same manner as did Herbert Hoover, who was for many years an executive in the Kaiping mines in China, where he discovered that "the disregard for human life permits cheap mining," and where he said that it was cheaper to pay 30

Mexican dollars for killing "an occasional Chinaman" than to timber the mines.[1]

"Furthermore, Mr. Hoover actually helped promote one company, the Irtysh Corporation, a year before the war began, and it was a concern which employed 3,000 Austrian prisoners of war as forced laborers." [2]

In 1904, the Chinese Engineering and Mining Company, under Mr. Hoover's management, accepted a contract for recruiting and shipping Chinese coolies to work in the mines of South Africa. The company undertook to ship 200,000 of these contract laborers who were recruited by fraudulent advertisements. Out of the very first shipment 51 workers died or jumped overboard. They were shipped at the rate of 2,000 per shipload in vessels that by regulation were only allowed to carry 1,000.[3]

In the Patino tin mines of Bolivia owned by Mr. Hoover's friends, the Guggenheims, we find semi-slave conditions existing among the Indians. These Indians are taken forcibly from their villages, transported in hordes to the tin mines where they work under contract for periods ranging from 16 to 24 hours at a stretch. After a few years in the mines they are broken down with tuberculosis and are discharged for inability to work. They then return to their villages where they die slowly of the plague contracted in the mines of the imperialists.

The semi-feudal government of Venezuela, supported by warships from Washington in the interests of the Mellon oil concessions, likewise employs forced labor. Peons and political prisoners are forced to work in the construction of roads and in the native *haciendas* of the bloody President Gomez.

FORCED LABOR IN THE WEST INDIES

Let us now consider some of the leading countries in which Yankee imperialism, by an even more direct control than in South America, piles up profits through the use of forced labor. Take first the group of islands in the Caribbean Sea, gateway to Latin America, including Cuba, Haiti, the Dominican Republic, Porto Rico and the Virgin Islands. Wall Street dominates throughout this area.[4]

Cuba was formerly a country of small farms, producing chiefly for local markets. To-day its main product is sugar, raised on great plantations, with an occasional sugar factory attached. This change was brought about through the virtual annexation of the country by American investors.

It has been estimated that over 85% of Cuba's arable land constitutes the sugar companies' domain and nothing but sugar is allowed to be planted on this land. Thus the means of subsistence have been taken from the natives and forced labor has been one of the inevitable results of this change. The brutality with which the native small landholders are being dispossessed is described in an article in *Current History,* November, 1930, by Charles W. Hackett, professor of Latin American History at the University of Texas. He says:

A clash occurred between citizens and troops on Sept. 19 at Sagua de Tanamo, Oriente Province, when Cuban soldiers arrested 37 residents, who were accused of fomenting a disturbance after more than 4,000 persons were ordered to move from the land of the Atlantic Fruit and Sugar Company, which they claimed was government-owned and on which they declared they had lived for 50 years.

In October, 1931, the small landowners in Cuba demanded a moratorium saying that their lands were rapidly passing into the hands of foreigners. Most of these lands are mortgaged to American capitalists. Interest rates to the small landowners range from 8 to 12%.*

* New York *Times,* October 19, 1931. The *Times* of November 29, 1931, reported that 30,912 eviction notices were filed in six municipal courts during the first six months of 1931. The last half of the year was expected to show a still greater increase.

IMPORTED FORCED LABOR IN CUBA

From the very beginning of the sugar industry the Cuban toilers struggled against their exploiters. They refused to accept the 20 cents a day which was often offered to laborers, and so the sugar companies hit upon the expedient of importing Negro workers from neighboring countries as was done in the days before slavery was legally abolished. The traffic in black workers proved so profitable that it has been continued to the present day. Arnold Roller, a first hand investigator of Cuban conditions, describes this slave trading in an article in *The Nation,* January 9, 1929:

Cuba's white gold, the source of its "national prosperity," depends for its future rôle in the national economy of the country on the size of its black population. The blacker Cuba becomes, the more white sugar will it be able to pour out in competition with the rest of the world. The production of sugar in Cuba depends entirely on black labor, most of it imported from Haiti, Jamaica, and the other Antilles, in a form which differs from the old slave traffic only by a few legalistic formalities. The Negroes are brought to Cuba in ships equipped as the slave ships of old and delivered for a premium of $15 to $20 each to the sugar companies on the basis of labor contracts signed by the Negroes with a finger-print.

It is easy for the sugar companies to circumvent the laws against forced labor with this fiction of a contract made with illiterate Negroes who do not understand the language of the country to which they are brought.

As recent examples, Roller cited the cases of such big American corporations as the United Fruit Co., which have "made their own laws, disregarding Cuban laws, and are establishing a kind of industrial extra-territoriality." These companies improved upon the ancient slave-trading methods. The General Sugar Co. stimulated the trade by paying $25 for every Negro delivered on its reservations, in addition to a small bonus.

Once in Cuba the Negroes are kept as virtual prisoners

on the reservations until the crop is gathered. They are imprisoned in large, wooden barracks surrounded by armed guards. They cannot leave the company's reservation during the entire time of their contract. They must buy all their provisions in company stores. Usually at the end of the crop they are indebted to the contractor. Often, after the season is over, the masters "allow" them to remain in the barracks, without having to pay rent, where they are kindly "protected" by armed company guards who shoot any one trying to escape. Thus the company saves the additional expense of importing new workers for the next season's work.

Since this modern slave traffic began the influx of Haitians and Jamaicans under contract labor has increased considerably. In 1912 less than 1,000 entered Cuba; in 1920, 63,000; in 1921 about 25,000. There was a big drop to 5,000 in 1922, a year of crisis in the sugar industry. The importation was resumed, however, and in 1924 the number rose to 26,000, falling to 17,000 in 1927. The Cuban government recently granted the United Fruit Co. permission to import 9,600 Negroes for its Cuban plantations. Under the arrangement made with this company, in order to get around the laws, a bond of $25 on each worker must be posted with the local authorities at each plantation district to guarantee that the Negro will be shipped back home when his term of employment ceases. Since it is cheaper to forfeit this small bond than to return the laborers and then import new ones, the local authorities are allowed to pocket the defaulted bonds!

During the current economic crisis fewer Negro contract laborers are being imported. However, Harvey O'Connor, *Federated Press* correspondent, wrote from Cuba, March 20, 1930: "These companies intensify the chronic unemployment on the island by importing Negro laborers—under slave terms—from Haiti and Santo Domingo. *These are kept in semi-military compounds, guarded by troops and denied every civil liberty."*

With sugar suffering from the crisis, President Machado is helping to take the drop in sugar prices out of the living conditions of the workers and peasants. One-fifth of the sugar supply of the world is being produced in Cuba at one-fourth the cost of sugar produced elsewhere while the Cuban workers are in peonage and get only food for their work.

Paying workers only in food or grocery checks was prohibited by the Arteaga law some years ago, but on November 1, 1929, this law was repealed by Machado's personal decree. "Since then workers get less than horses—their fodder only and no care." [5]

The Cuban ruling class and the foreign capitalists have provided laws devised to prevent the forced laborers in Cuba from struggling against these conditions. The *Monthly Labor Review* of September, 1929, discusses Article 268 of the Penal Code which provides "indirectly for the punishment of strikes on farms, declaring that 'those who disturb the public peace in order to create prejudice against any individual shall be punished.' The same penalty is provided for persons who cause trouble or who seriously attempt to disturb the order on farms by unwillingness to work, by disobeying, or by resisting the persons in charge of the management or administration."

Another way in which the government helps the sugar planters to take the fall in sugar prices out of the "hides" of the workers is shown in an order to all city police chiefs on January 21, 1931, by Captain Frederico Quintero, Military District Pinar del Rio:

Sir: The sugar harvest finding itself in full activity and it being a notorious fact that much of the available laboring force is showing a refusal to leave the city . . . to go to work cutting cane, which goes to prove a lamentable state of vagrancy. . . . This class of really despicable people that hates

work and order, you must notify that they have to go into cane
cutting or, if not, to abandon the place where they wish to live
without working. . . . As soon as you have rounded up the
vagrants and parasites of the city you belong to, you must
reach an agreement with the various labor contractors of the
sugar mills for the supply to them of the men you are able to
offer.
                    Yours respectfully,
             CAPTAIN FREDERICO QUINTERO, M.M.,
                    Cavalry Captain, National Army,
                    Provincial Supervisor,
                    Municipal Police Corps.

IN BLACK HAITI

The usual imperialist practice of robbing land from peasant owners has also operated in Haiti, a country long dominated by American bankers, coffee, sugar and fruit barons.
Despite Haitian laws much arable land has been taken over
by these American interests. The peasants must work under
forced labor conditions for Wall Street financial interests—
notably the National City Bank—or starve, as there is no
other way to earn a living.

One of the ways of getting the land in Haiti was to
demand of the peasant proprietors a deed showing owner-
ship. Such deeds cannot be produced because of the simple
fact that there are no such deeds in existence and never
have been. In 1804 the Haitian slaves rebelled, drove out
the French slaveholders, and confiscated the land. Naturally, under such circumstances, no deeds were needed. Writing of this method of robbing the land from the natives,
L. J. De Bekker, an authority on colonial matters, said:

No lessor can prove title under such land law as the Marine
Corps will understand, and when it comes to a showdown in the
new Tribunal de Cassation the peasant proprietors will find
that they have given up their birthrights . . . and will be lucky
to find work at 25 cents a day on what had been their own
property, inherited from father to son for more than a century
previous to the American occupation . . . these peasant proprietors, who will become laborers on their former possessions
or find themselves in the chain-gangs.[6]

The chief form of out-and-out forced labor in Haiti has been on road and construction work. Not being able to secure a sufficient supply of such labor by other means the Wall Street invaders under General John H. Russell and the U. S. Marine Corps, revived an ancient and obsolete Haitian law known as the *corvée*, which required that the natives work a certain number of days for the "government" building roads. While nominally this was work for the Haitian government it actually benefited the imperialists as it gave them military, business and pleasure roads.

Ernest H. Gruening, a well-known writer on this subject, describes the working of the *corvée* as enforced by the brutal U. S. Marines:

Testimony varies as to the extent of the abuses committed under the corvée, but it seems to be clearly proved that Haitians were (a) seized wherever they could be found; (b) transported to other parts of the island; (c) compelled to work under guard, often for weeks; (d) placed under guard at night to prevent their escape; (e) subjected to physical violence if they resisted; (f) shot if they attempted to escape. Navy Department testimony admits that at least a hundred were thus killed. Haitian figures are very much higher.[7]

In Central America

In the "independent" republics of Central America, dominated by American imperialism, forced labor is used in varying forms and under various names. Peonage, however, as we have indicated, is the most typical form. Indeed, the South and Central American countries are the traditional home of peonage. American capitalists who own vast sugar, banana, and chicle plantations in Central America are the foremost exploiters of this type of forced labor. They also dominate the public utilities, wharves, mines and other industries of the region.

The peons are mostly native Indians recruited with the aid of local authorities and political bosses for the large native and foreign landowners. Many imported Negroes are also held in peonage.   This is especially true in Costa Rica, Honduras and Panama, which are now populated in certain areas with Negroes imported by special labor contractors from the West Indies.

The peon is doubly exploited. Of the daily wages promised him at least two-thirds and often three-fourths is deducted by the landlord and paid out to the political boss and contractor. If anything is left after paying for his subsistence, the local authorities see to it that the peon if he is out of work again is fined for "vagrancy," to the full amount of his "savings." Or he may be arrested for "drunkenness" or "disorderly conduct."

Peonage in Guatemala

Conditions in Guatemala, where about 50 million dollars of United States capital are invested, are typical of those found in almost every Central American country. In Guatemala the system is quite open. Even the 1932 *World Almanac* admits that many of the Indians—who comprise about 60% of the population—are held "under a system of peonage." The *Monthly Labor Review* of May, 1930, quotes the International Labor Office as saying that the Guatemalan government is engaged in the forcible recruiting of labor for private undertakings.

The workers and peasants are held in bondage to the landowners and other employers through a system of debt. Dana G. Munro, Chief of the Division of Latin American Affairs of the U. S. State Department, writing about peonage in Guatemala, admits the operation of this system, describing it as follows:

The *jornaleros*, or day laborers, are held on the plantations under a peonage system. Theoretically the Indian is perfectly free to contract himself or not as he pleases, but when he has done so, he may not leave his employer's service until he has completed the time for which he has agreed to work and has repaid any money which the *patron* may have lent him. If he attempts to escape he is hunted down by the authorities and returned to the plantation; and the entire expense of capturing him and bringing him back is debited in his account. If, on the other hand, he refuses to work, he may be imprisoned until he is in a more reasonable frame of mind.

Those who still prove obstinate, after fifteen days in jail, may be sent at the request of the employer to the convict labor squads where fifty per cent of the returns of their labor are set aside for the benefit of the creditors. For this purpose he is allowed a limited amount of credit at the plantation store and is even loaned small sums of money from time to time . . . those who leave the plantation can only look forward to similar employment elsewhere, or what is much worse, to impressment into the army, from which *mozos* (laborers) working on large coffee, sugar-cane, banana, or cacao plantations are legally exempt.

. . . The combined earnings of the whole family, for the women and children are usually given tasks as well as the men, are in fact hardly sufficient to supply the necessities of life without an occasional extra loan from the employer. . . . Indians are often induced to sign contracts by misrepresentation or even actual violence. . . .

Many of the representatives of the government derive a large income from considerations paid them for service of this kind and from tributes which they exact every month or every year from the planters in their districts as the price of official support in disputes with their laborers.[8]

The symbol of bondage in Guatemala is a little book carried by every Indian worker, in which the "wages" and debts of the worker are recorded. For a work-day of 14 hours these workers usually receive from two and a half to eight cents. In the cover of the book is the copy of a contract in which the peon agrees to work off all debts and fees before quitting employment and agrees not to accept work elsewhere. He agrees also not to leave for any reason without permission. Workers are charged for nearly every conceivable item including the fee to the labor contractor, tools, clothing and fines. Their land having been stolen they are forced to accept any employment offered or starve. One of these little books recently examined shows that a worker who escaped from a plantation actually earned $88.07

from October, 1920, to February, 1930! With such incredibly low wages the worker is forced deeper and deeper into debt and servitude. Even children are sometimes held in peonage to pay a dead parent's debt. The value of a plantation is often estimated on the basis of the number of contract laborers on it.

In Guatemala, as in other Central American countries, dominated by United States imperialism, concessions to foreign capitalists often stipulate that the government shall supply the necessary labor. Guillermo Rodriguez describes the resulting forced labor in his book, *Guatemala:*

And even more abusive and habitual is the arrival of the mounted and infantry escorts to capture the workers; by day and by night in their homes or at their work, without asking permission of any one, they hunt them down like deer, they are caught, bound and carried off.[9]

A document of greater authority, and more conservative than any we have quoted on Latin American affairs, is *Tropical Agriculture,* official organ of the Imperial College of Tropical Agriculture in Trinidad. Regarding Guatemala, it says in its issue of August, 1924:

A sufficient number of laborers for routine work live in settlements on the estates; but at picking time larger numbers are required, and the agents enlist them in the villages of the interior by means of advances. . . . They are nearly all kept in debt for control purposes. If there is any difficulty in recruiting labor for picking, the Guatemalan officials force the laborers under threat of conscription in the army, or even impressment.

LIBERIA—A RUBBER COLONY

In Liberia, on the west coast of Africa, we find United States imperialism benefiting by a still more terrible type of forced labor. In this case there is actual chattel slavery—the buying and selling of human beings as property. Liberia was founded as a free Negro republic in 1822 to serve as a "haven" for Negro freedmen from the United States. To-day it has a population estimated at between two, and

two and a half million. Over 15,000 are "Americo-Liberians," that is, descendants of immigrants from the United
States. The remainder are native Liberians.

In return for a loan to the Liberian government the
Firestone Rubber Co. secured a concession of 1,000,000
acres of rubber land in 1925. This deal was pushed through
with the aid of Herbert Hoover, who was then engaged,
as U. S. Secretary of Commerce, in breaking the British
rubber monopoly. The land given Firestone had formerly
been held by natives but it was taken from them without
asking their views in the matter.

In carrying through its large-scale plantations project the
Firestone company has been confronted with two major
problems: (1) confiscation of native lands, and (2) an adequate supply of cheap labor. The Liberian government,
then headed by President King, actively coöperated in solv-
ing both. The land was expropriated and attempts of the
natives to escape labor on the plantations were defeated by
terroristic methods. Not only did the government supply
Firestone with forced laborers, but it supplied other imperialists operating in other parts of Africa with such labor.

The Liberian slave trade recently became such an international scandal that even the League of Nations was forced
to make a gesture of protest. An international commission
of three members was appointed to look into the matter.
The commission made its report in 1930. Among the serious charges to be investigated were the use of forced labor
on roads for nine months in the year and the selling of
slaves to the near-by Spanish colony of Fernando Po. The
investigating commission reported that slavery as described
in the 1926 anti-slavery convention of the League of Nations
does exist in Liberia. "Pawning" was found to exist.
Pawning is defined as "an old native custom which is sub-
stantially an arrangement by which for a money return a
human being, ordinarily a child relative, is placed in servitude indefinitely without pay or privilege." The commission

found evidence that Americo-Liberians often used female pawns to attract male laborers to their land.

A large percentage of the contract laborers shipped from Liberia to Spanish Fernando Po, to work on cocoa plantations, and to French Gabun were found to be recruited under conditions similar to slave raiding. Forty-five dollars for each "boy" was paid to Liberian officials plus a bonus of $5,000 for each 1,500 shipped, the report declared. The Vice-President and other high officials of the Liberian government, including county superintendents and district commissioners, have sanctioned the compulsory recruiting of laborers "and have condoned this use of force . . . to convoy gangs of captured natives to the coast and to guard them there up to the time of their shipment." When native chiefs could supply no more "boys" they were heavily fined and even flogged.

It was also found that the government gave authorization to the use of forced laborers on private plantations. Vice-President Yancy, President King and several commissioners were found to be using such slaves on their own estates. A great variety of work was found to be performed by forced labor, which was mainly used for the construction of motor roads, for building military barracks, civil compounds, and other construction. It was used also for porterage and on private plantations. None of these workers were paid. On the contrary. In Maryland—a Liberian province—some of the workers were compelled to pay large amounts to the owners of plantations to obtain their release from a term of unpaid and unfed labor. The workers were required to feed themselves and furnish their own tools.[10]

The League commission, however, found no "evidence that the Firestone Plantations Co. consciously employs any but voluntary labor on its leased rubber plantations." But the commission's work may not have been so "impartial" as it pretended to be. For in the preface to its findings it profusely thanked "Mr. W. D. Hines and the Firestone Co.

for valuable transport and other facilities much appreciated by the Commissioners." In other words, this commission, appointed to investigate Firestone's use of forced labor, went to Liberia and put itself in the hands of Firestone and was shown about the country by his agents.

In the concession given to Firestone by the Liberian government the latter agreed to guarantee an adequate supply of "suitable" labor. In discussing this point, R. L. Buell of the Foreign Policy Association says:

Agreement Number Two provides that the Liberian government will "encourage, support and assist the efforts of the Lessee to secure and maintain an adequate Labor supply." . . . In the spring of 1926 the government established this Labor Bureau at the head of which it appointed a Commissioner, under the control of the Secretary of the Interior. According to this Commissioner, the Bureau will supply annually a total of 10,000 men to the Firestone Plantations—two thousand men from each county. By June, 1926, the Bureau already had supplied the Plantations with six hundred men. It sent out requisitions to each Native and District Commissioner who in turn divided up contingents among the chiefs. According to the Commissioner, the Firestone Plantations paid the chiefs one cent a day for each boy, and the same sum to the Government Bureau.

Thus, under this system, which is similar to that which has produced wholesale compulsory labor in other parts of Africa, the Firestone Plantations Company is making it financially worth while for the government and for the chiefs to keep the plantations supplied. . . . As Liberian officials and chiefs are already accustomed to imposing compulsion whether in securing men for road work or for Fernando Po, there is no reason to believe that they will employ any different methods in obtaining labor for the Firestone Plantations. . . .[11]

President King, who was found to be a slave-dealer and exploiter, worked hand in hand with Firestone and their pictures were frequently taken together. Lester A. Walton quotes President King as saying in his 1929 message to the legislature: "Through Mr. W. D. Hines, Mr. Firestone's personal representative in Liberia, and a gentleman of most charming personality, the most cordial relations have been maintained between the government and the company. . . ." [12]

One native worker who testified before the commission said he would rather go to Fernando Po, with all its horrors, than to Firestone's "where payment is too small because they pay us one shilling a day and out of that daily shilling you have to get your daily bread. . . ." Workers complained that "we got nothing when Firestone took our land. This year we will have no rice because Firestone took our land."

Firestone hired the conscripted laborers and politely asked no questions. In return the government was often allowed to collect the workers' wages and to tax them. Naturally the company is too clever to have it appear on its books that the laborers are slaves.

Aside from its actual plantation work, the Firestone company used forced labor indirectly. One of the main obstacles to the exploitation of the country was the lack of transportation facilities. The only means of communication between the inland sections and the seaports were mud paths with no bridges over streams. Large-scale American efficiency production of rubber was impossible under such conditions. So Firestone insisted on making a big loan to the government, stipulating that a large part of the loan was to go to building roads and similar public improvements. Forced labor was used in constructing these roads and in other public works beneficial to the Firestone interests.

In the face of these facts, and in the face of the complete domination of the country by Firestone, the League commission found that Firestone did not "consciously use forced labor." Actually, of course, Firestone and the United States government are as responsible for these slavery conditions as are their puppets—the Liberian officials. When Secretary of State Stimson learned that the commission would report findings of forced labor, he came out as a great "humanitarian." He sent a "sharp note" to the Liberian government condemning forced labor, but joined in the deception that Firestone was innocent of engaging in the traffic.

As after all white-wash "investigations" nothing was done for the sufferers. On the contrary, an observer who was in Liberia in 1931 found that none of the Liberian officials, including President King and Vice-President Yancy, had ever been arrested or brought to trial for their proved participation in the slave traffic. Yancy was still living like a feudal lord on his plantation near Cape Palmos. This investigator also found that workers who testified before the League commission had been victimized. He reported a prospering slave industry still in full blast. His findings are supported by a cable from Geneva to the New York *Times*, January 23, 1932, which reads:

> Liberian natives who testified before the League of Nations Commission which inquired into reports of slavery and economic conditions in the Negro republic have been visited by severe reprisals, representatives of humanitarian organizations reported to-day.
>
> Homes have been burned, they said, and even whole villages of those who reported to the League on the labor situation in the republic have been destroyed.

Even the Liberian government admits that 44 villages have been burned and 81 men, 49 women and 29 children killed. Many of these were burned to death. The net result of the League's investigation, aside from persecuting the natives and white-washing the Firestone Co., has been to prepare the ground for a stricter control of Liberia by Firestone. The latest move of the League, on the suggestion of Stimson, is the proposal of a plan to appoint a foreign "advisor" with absolute dictatorial powers over the country in the interest of Firestone.

CONTRACT LABOR IN HAWAII

The recent Massie trial in Hawaii has served to emphasize the stranglehold of the United States over these islands in the Pacific, so indispensable as a naval base and as a source of profit to the imperialists from the American mainland. American capitalists are the beneficiaries of the near-feudal system that cruelly exploits the natives and the labor imported into these islands.

Workers were imported to work the plantations of Hawaii as early as the 1860's. During a period of 20 years, 1865 to 1886, over 33,000 Chinese coolie contract laborers were brought in. One writer on Hawaii says that between 1877 and 1890 some 55,000 immigrant laborers were imported. They came under contracts which were to pay them an average of $4 monthly, but that does not mean they received that much in actual cash.

A writer in *Asia* shows that this importation of contract labor is going on even during the present economic crisis. Although workers in Hawaii are unemployed the sugar companies are constantly in the market for cheaper labor and are importing from 100 to 300 Filipinos every two weeks.[18]

To insure a constant supply of cheap labor about 50 sugar companies united to form the Sugar Planters' Association whose chief duty is to insure contract labor for member plantations. Regular solicitors travel from country to country, especially in Porto Rico and the Philippines, attempting to entice workers to the "Pearl of the Pacific." After workers arrive in Hawaii they are told that their contracts specify that they must work three years, 20 days a month and 10 hours a day. The contract also forbids the worker to leave the plantation to which he is assigned until at least one year has elapsed.

Overseers on the Hawaiian sugar plantations have stated that:

If a contract laborer is idling in the fields we dock him; we give him only one-half to three-fourths of a day, and if he keeps it up we resort to the law and have him arrested for refusing to work. For the first offense he is ordered back to work and he has to pay the costs of court. If he refuses to

obey orders, he is arrested again and a light fine inflicted which
the planter can pay and take it out of his pay, or else he is
put on the road. For the third offense he is likely to get three
months' imprisonment.

In 1920, following a strike of Japanese workers on the
Hawaiian plantations, the Sugar Planters' Association tried
to secure permission from the United States Congress to
import Chinese, regardless of immigration restrictions. Failing in this they began to import Filipinos. In connection
with this attempt to import Chinese laborers even the conservative *Washington Times* was forced to say:

> The House Committee on Immigration has reported a most
> extraordinary resolution in favor of permitting the planters of
> Hawaii to import 50,000 Chinese coolies to work as bonded
> slaves on the sugar plantations for five years, and then, if de-
> sirable, to be deported in favor of another batch.[14]

This has always been the policy of the rich sugar planters.
They import illiterate laborers and when the latter discover
after their arrival in Hawaii that they are held in peonage,
they go on strike. The planters then proceed to import new
workers whom they attempt to use as strike-breakers. Following the strike of Japanese workers in 1920—between
1922 and 1929—66,184 Filipinos were imported.[15]

In the words of a Filipino labor leader, the life of the
"plantation workers in the Hawaiian islands is a series of
long days of strenuous toil, under the blazing heat of the
equatorial sun, at a salary that is often too low for the
most vital material necessities." Even during the pre-crisis
days of 1929, male workers, who were in the overwhelming
majority, earned on the average $11.04 a week while the
women averaged only $7.80, according to the United States
Bureau of Labor Statistics. No extra rate was paid for
overtime.

But to understand what such figures mean it is necessary
to know that Hawaii imports a large proportion of its total
food supply since most of its farm land is planted with

money crops and very little foodstuff is raised. The distance between Hawaii and the mainland of the United States is so great that the cost of importing food and other necessities adds greatly to the price of these commodities. Thus low wages must meet very high prices. The result is that the workers are forced to live largely on rice.

PEONAGE IN THE PHILIPPINES

American capitalists have invested over $400,000,000 in the Philippine Islands, the most important possession of the United States in the Orient. In this country, as in all other colonies, a wide expropriation of the peasants' land has taken place, although probably 90% of the masses are dependent upon agriculture for a livelihood. Over 325 plantations ranging from 1,500 to 25,000 acres each are operated in the Philippines. Around 2,000,000 tenants and farm laborers are employed on them. The process of extending the large landholdings is still going on and it is only logical to expect that eventually the situation will be like that in Cuba where American sugar corporations have swallowed up all the best sugar lands.

A leading United States business journal, in describing the life on the big rice plantations, cynically remarked: "It is feudal farming; the manager is the manor laird, and these his tenants his fief lieges." [16] The rich landlords usually contrive to involve their tenants and farm laborers in debt. They cannot leave their employment until the debt is paid. Interest rates range from 10 to 20% a month.

In describing the peonage which is the most important type of forced labor in the Philippines, Dean C. Worcester, a leading authority, said:

The rich and powerful man, commonly known as the *cacique,* encourages the poor man to borrow money from him under such conditions that the debt can never be repaid, and holds the debtor and frequently the members of his family as well in debt servitude for life. One might fill a score of volumes with records of such cases. . . . Peonage is so common and wide-spread that it may be called general. . . . It lies at the very root of the industrial system of the Philippines.*

Writing in 1928, Dr. Robert W. Hart, of the United States Public Health Service, stationed in the Philippines for many years, declared in *The Philippines Today* (p. 154 *ff*):

As a matter of fact, borne out by my own investigations and those of others, a comparatively small proportion of laborers in the rural districts receive any compensation whatsoever other than the right to a mere existence. . . .

Usury, regardless of all laws to the contrary, is universal in the islands and, of course, the more ignorant the poor Tao, caught in the clutches of the landholder, the more difficult it is for him to get free. . . . As he is ignorant, not only of financial matters, but of his legal rights as well, this note [money borrowed from a landlord] is held over his head week after week, month after month, and year after year, always drawing an excessive rate of interest, and on numerous occasions the interest on the loan amounts to ten or more times the original principal. In lieu of actually paying such a debt in cash, it is no infrequent occurrence for the laborer to "bind out" either himself or the members of his family for an indefinite period, to cover it. As a result, while slavery and peonage do not legally exist in the islands, the end result is actually the same.

Necessarily, no figures are available on the subject [peonage], nor is there any way of obtaining exact information regarding it. The landlord, of course, makes no mention of it, and the poor illiterate, ignorant Tao, as well as his family, are held in such abject terror . . . that even should the investigator be able to speak their language and become well acquainted, the condition is never admitted, through fear of the consequences. . . .

It is estimated that no less than 20% of the total laboring population of the islands are held in practical slavery. It is true that the laborers have freedom to come and go, to associate with whom they please, to marry, to raise children and to live, yet they are essentially slaves, toiling from early morning until late at night at the will of their masters to whom they are in debt.

* Dean C. Worcester, *Philippines, Past and Present,* pp. 534-535. In 1914, says Worcester, three members of the Filipino legislature were found to be holding workers in peonage. Both houses of the legislature are made up of the *cacique* class.

A special Mission on Investigation to the Philippine Islands, reported October 8, 1921, that:

> A frequent cause of complaint is against extreme action taken under the provisions of Act 2098, which enables employers of labor to prosecute their laborers for a breach of contract, and in many cases to hold them against their will, resulting in a kind of legalized peonage. . . . Under the provisions of this act, should they leave before completion of contract they can be arrested and tried for violation of contract and for obtaining money or supplies under false pretenses. During the fiscal year 1918 there was a total of 3,266 cases of this nature.

Struggles Against Forced Labor in the Colonies

None of the colonial revolts against United States imperialism have been more significant than those in the Philippines. After fighting a desperate guerilla warfare for 15 years the Moros (Mohammedan peasants) were practically annihilated by the United States and native troops trained by American officers. In the battles of Bud Daho and Bagstad, waged in 1906 and 1913 respectively, the women fought alongside the men. It has been estimated that on the Island of Luzon alone hundreds of thousands of women and children have been slaughtered by American soldiers or died as the result of the Wall Street wars of conquest.[17]

There have been many rebellions recently against the same oppression in the Philippines. There was an uprising of the Tayug peasants in January, 1931. Hundreds of men and women armed only with clubs and cane knives marched into the town of Tayug, Pagasinian province. They set out for their direct exploiters, those who collected the taxes. In spite of the fact that the workers had no guns they were fired upon. One was killed, whereupon the angry peasants and laborers killed a lieutenant and several soldiers who were responsible. A pitched battle ensued lasting two days.

A sympathetic soldier helped the rebels break into the storeroom where arms and ammunition were kept. After they were thus armed, they took over the city of 15,000 inhabitants and held it for several days. All deeds and records of mortgages were burned. The movement was entirely spontaneous. The immediate cause of the Tayug uprising was the decision of the Philippine Supreme Court which legalized the seizure of land belonging to 1,000 peasants by the foreign-owned Esperanza estate which already contained 100,000 acres.

The revolt was finally crushed. Four men and two women were killed. Caesare Abe and Pedro Kalosa, leaders, were given life imprisonment. Of the others, 37 were condemned to 17 years' imprisonment, and two to 14 years, among them two less than 15 years of age. Two judges, an American and a Filipino—symbolic of the unity between Wall Street and the Filipino ruling class—handed down the sentences.

To hide the real cause of this uprising it was called "a revolt of religious fanatics." The capitalist press said it was a revolt of "Colorums," suggesting a mystical religious sect. While the revolt was being crushed, the peasants were called "bandits." This is the stock label now used by the imperialists to designate all those who oppose their rule and who are, therefore, marked for persecution and slaughter.

On January 13, 1931, the New York *Times* reported threatened uprisings in the towns of Santa Maria, Umingan and Rosales, while the public peace in Nueva Ecija Province was regarded as "none too secure." August 13, 1931, the *Times* reported another uprising of peasants in the same section. "Reports from Nueva Ecja, which is the center of the disturbance, say that the uprising is . . . aimed . . . against rich Filipinos, who are charged with oppressing the poor. Many of the wealthy landlords have rushed to Manila. . . . Land and credit abuses are believed responsible for discontent in Central Luzon. . . ."

On March 15, 1932, the same paper reported that 125 Tangulan peasants were sentenced to imprisonment of from one to six years, in addition to being assessed fines ranging from $100 to $1,000 each. They were charged with "conspiracy to commit rebellion."

But the Philippines is not the only colony, protectorate or "sphere of influence" of Wall Street where revolts have broken out against forms of forced labor.

We can make here only brief reference to a few of these struggles. Many strikes have been fought in the Hawaiian Islands, especially by the imported Japanese workers in 1920 and by the Filipinos in 1924. During the latter strike at least 15 Filipino workers were murdered by police; many were railroaded to prison at hard labor. The sugar companies had special police in their pay.

There have been revolts also in Haiti, arising largely over the *corvée* law. Even the officials of the United States Marine Corps are forced to admit that 3,250 Haitian peasants were killed either by the marines or by the marine-trained native troops in "pacifying" the country. General Barnett, commander of the Marine Corps, admitted that "practically indiscriminate killing of natives had been going on for some time." [18]

There have been also many fights against forced labor and imperialism in Cuba, carried on especially by the agricultural workers on the sugar plantations. Big strikes were waged in 1906, 1920, 1925, 1926, and in more recent years. During the 1925 and 1926 strikes hundreds of workers and peasants were slaughtered. Only a few years ago 60 Canary Island farm laborers were hung in Cuba at one time after the disappearance of a Camaguey army colonel and plantation owner who never paid his workers. [19]

In the past 25 years thousands of poor farmers and workers in Cuba have been murdered and more than 5,000 arrested chiefly on the orders of the big American corporations and their local agents.

But in spite of all this repression the Cuban workers and peasants are now moving in a new revolutionary wave, and they are showing that they have learned from the past. The bloody battles in Havana streets on December 14, 1929; the political strike of January 10, 1930; the general strike of some 200,000 persons, March 30, 1930, against unemployment and against the persecution of the unions; the demonstrations on May 1; the strike of over 15,000 tobacco workers which was betrayed by the reformist leaders; the strikes of the street car men and sugar workers—most of them led by the National Workers' Federation of Cuba and the Communist Party—these mark a long and persistent struggle against imperialist exploitation with its attendant forced labor.

In many countries of Central and South America there have been recent uprisings against forced labor and oppression.

In Guatemala, for example, spontaneous revolts of the Indian peons take the form of mass burning of their slave books in which their perpetual debts are recorded. These books, which are the symbol of forced labor, are bitterly hated by the workers who express their rebellion frequently by burning them.

The extent of forced labor in Colombia was disclosed by the great strike of the banana workers of the United Fruit Co., in the district of Santa Marta in 1928, when over 1,500 men, women and children were murdered by troops. These Colombian laborers had been held virtually prisoners on the banana plantations and were not allowed to leave even for a short time. Workers were given only 60% of their wages, the rest were held at the local offices of this American company as a guarantee that the workers would not escape. The workers were often flogged when they tried to escape or did not do enough work. They live in company houses; buy food from company stores; are paid in scrip, and work from sun to sun. While the troops were suppressing the strike, two United States warships were anchored off Colombia ready to give aid when needed. The whole brutal suppression occurred at the orders of the United Fruit Co., backed by Washington.

CHAPTER IX

"FORCED LABOR" IN THE SOVIET UNION

YEAR after year the capitalist world has watched the workers of the Soviet Union speeding industrialization under the stimulus of the first Five-Year Plan. As the country of socialism gained in power and in the sympathy of the world proletariat, the economic crisis was developing disastrously in the rest of the world—at least 40 million workers unemployed, every country facing financial bankruptcy and an acute sharpening of the class struggle. The capitalists saw ruin for their social system unless something was done and that soon. But what could be done? And they asked:

Cannot we settle this or that contradiction of capitalism, or all the contradictions taken together, at the expense of the U.S.S.R., the land of the Soviets, the citadel of the revolution, revolutionizing by its very existence the working class and the colonies, preventing us arranging for a new war, preventing us dividing the world anew, preventing us being masters of our own extensive internal market, so necessary for capitalists, particularly to-day, in connection with the economic crisis?[1]

The capitalists have answered this question in the affirmative. Yes, it would help stabilize capitalism if the Soviet Union were destroyed. It would be a crushing blow to the working class internationally, the capitalists reason. Hence we find the tendency to sporadic armed assaults on the U.S.S.R. which the capitalists hope will lead to armed intervention, a tendency which becomes stronger daily as the economic crisis deepens.

The capitalist world has thus felt an urgent need to create a sentiment for war against the Soviet Union and to try to prevent the successful completion of the Five-Year Plans. To this end it has tried many devices. But so far every

weapon used against the Soviet Union has proved a boomer-
ang. One of the first charges was that in the Soviet Union
"women were being nationalized." That lie blew up quickly.
Then the cry of "Russian oil" was raised. But the Soviet
workers answered the challenge by completing the Five-Year
Plan in oil production in only two and a half years. Next
the British Tories unearthed the fake "Zinoviev letter" which
resulted in temporary severance of trade relations between
England and the Soviet Union.

Then in the United States the lurid "Whalen Documents"
were put out by New York's fashion-plate Police Commissioner, Grover A. Whalen. They were intended to link the
Amtorg Trading Corporation (Soviet trade agency in the
United States) with "revolutionary propaganda." But an
alert newspaperman discovered that these "documents," alleged to have been printed in the Soviet Union, were actually
forged by monarchist Russians in a small print shop on the
East Side of New York City.[2] Finally, big business internationally was able to overcome partisan religious lines and
Catholics, led by the Pope, Jews and Protestants went into
a huddle. Out of this conspiracy of church and business
came the accusation that the workers of the Soviet Union
were "spitting on God." This attack, based on the contention
that "believers" were persecuted in the Soviet Union, started
off with a bang. It soon collapsed of its own weight.

The latest charge—with which this chapter is concerned—
is that of "dumping." But on second thought the capitalists
saw that this charge by itself could not hold water. After
all, they were forced to admit to themselves, dumping is a
regular capitalist practice. So the charge of dumping was
changed to "dumping of goods produced by convicts and other
forced labor."

Who Charges Soviet Forced Labor?

So for the past two years or more a scurrilous campaign
has been conducted by the capitalist world against "forced

labor" in the Soviet Union. This has been an international campaign. The House of Lords in England; the Congress of the United States; the French Parliament; journalists, socialists and bankers, archbishops and rabbis, patrioteers and captains of industry all reëchoed this charge. The same capitalists who lead this attack have a most unsavory record, as we have shown, since forced labor is a phenomenon of capitalism just as it was of feudalism and other social systems. The capitalists were silent when the Tsar held the great mass of the Russian people in serfdom. They secured Allied intervention in Russia and helped finance white guards in their attempt to overthrow the Soviets. Among the many socialist "friends of the workers" who joined in the campaign were Karl Kautsky, whom Lenin called the renegade, and Rafael Abramovitch, the Russian Menshevik. In fact the whole Second (Socialist) International participated in this new attack upon the Soviet Republic.

The attack has been especially venomous in the United States. In this country the "Fish Committee" (Special Committee to Investigate Communist Activities and Propaganda in the United States), the National Lumber Manufacturers' Association, the American Manganese Producers' Association, anthracite coal producers, the top leadership of the American Federation of Labor, the National Civic Federation —the latter two outfits being represented prominently by Matthew Woll—the American Legion and the Daughters of the American Revolution have been most active.

For a time it looked as if the campaign would be successful in wiping out Soviet-American trade—and it was successful to a large degree. Largely through this campaign a provision was put into the Smoot-Hawley tariff act of 1930 forbidding importation of goods produced by convicts or by any other form of forced labor. Ostensibly a general measure applying to any country, the real purpose of the bill was to destroy the market for Soviet goods. This is evidenced partly by the many efforts to get a law passed specifically banning all

Soviet products without even the pretext of "forced labor." It was thought that since this country had no diplomatic relations with the U.S.S.R. no evidence would be produced exposing the charges of forced labor.

Under this statutory provision the Treasury Department, which has jurisdiction over its enforcement, temporarily held up several cargoes of Soviet pulp-wood imports on the pretext that the wood was suspected of having been produced by convict labor.

Subsequently, the Treasury Department held hearings on the matter and was forced to admit that the evidence submitted to support the charges of convict labor was "conflicting and inconclusive," and it, therefore, had to lift the embargo. This was the first time the false charges were ever reviewed by an official body. However, the threat of the law is ever present as each cargo is passed upon separately and there is no telling just when the Treasury Department will cause expense and delay by stopping another shipment.

Some of the Charges

Timber experts who analyzed the specific charges of the manufacturers of "forced labor" myths in connection with Soviet timber found them to be false on their face. For instance, it was found that two alleged timber centers, where convicts were supposed to be employed in cutting wood for export, did not exist at all!

One absurd charge was that prisoners were forced to work 16 to 18 hours a day and to begin work in the forest so early that matches had to be used in searching for the trees to be cut! Actually, as experts pointed out, in the northern districts during the felling season the maximum daylight lasts six hours and therefore if this were true the prisoners would have to fell trees from 10 to 12 hours in darkness. Any logger knows this would be practically impossible and altogether impractical. The trees must be so cut that they will fall where they can be trimmed and handled easily. In order to throw the tree in the desired spot it is necessary to have adequate light to judge the way it leans and the position of other trees. If the tree falls in the wrong direction and hits other trees, much timber is needlessly ruined.

Another statement was that each prisoner must fell a total of 44 trees a day. If this were true it would take only 10,000 men, working 90 days, to produce all the timber that is exported annually from the Soviet Union! But look at the next charge. According to one statement, May 1, 1930, there were 662,000 prisoners producing timber in concentration camps. At the work rate given above these would produce more than 100 times the total sawed timber exported. Another "affidavit" gave a still more impossible figure of 55 to 60 trees a day. These trees, according to the same charge, must be cut at soil level—this in winter and with several feet of snow! Another wild rumor had it that 5,000,000 kulaks had been sent to timber cutting in the north country. But, as a matter of fact, in 1931, there were only 1,134,000 workers in the entire lumber industry.

At another time an accusation was made that 60,000 prisoners were toiling in two timber cutting camps. But timber experts point out that lumber camps of 30,000 or even 3,000 men cannot exist. Operations on so vast a scale would be impossible, for all the timber for miles around would soon be used up. Another "affidavit" alleged that 500 convicts were being used to load each small vessel. Those acquainted with timber shipping know that this too must be untrue. No more than 60 to 70 men can be engaged in loading one such ship. There were many other similar inconsistencies in this organized campaign of "revelation," exaggeration and lying.

THE ANSWER TO THE CHARGES

Dozens of statements were made by European and American authorities, all of them voluntary, refuting the charge of the use of convict and other forced labor in timber cutting. These statements are from capitalist and liberal as well as working class sources.

In a letter dated January 29, 1931, Danishevsky, chairman of Exportles (the organization in charge of all Soviet timber exports), said:

> . . . I am in possession of the most complete and up-to-date information; and I am in a position to state that *not a single standard of timber exported from the Soviet Union is produced otherwise than on conditions established by collective agreements* between the trade unions representing the workers and the State timber-producing trusts. Neither in the felling and preparing of timber for export nor in the loading of it into ships is labor allowed on any other conditions than those based on voluntary contracts and collective agreements. The collective agreements which were in force last year assured the workers of a wage double that of pre-war days. . . . It is ridiculous to represent the enrolment of these workers as anything approaching compulsory recruiting, whereby workers from far-distant localities are forcibly driven to the extreme north. The influx of workers to the timber regions is a permanent phenomenon, which was as common in pre-war Russia as it is to-day, and is an important source of income to the peasantry of vast regions in the country. The only difference in this respect is that the wages and conditions of labor are now incomparably better than they were then. . . .[3]

Lumberjacks from Finland, Canada and various other countries, now working in the Soviet Union, have added their protest to that of workers everywhere at the attack on the Five-Year Plan. Even several influential British labor leaders, some of them members of Parliament in 1931, have admitted that the charges of forced labor in the Soviet Union were false and aimed at the defeat of the Five-Year Plan. Among them were J. Bromley, M.P., secretary of the Associated Societies of Locomotive Engineers and Firemen; Alfred M. Wall, secretary of the London Trades Council; A. A. Purcell of the Manchester and Salford Trades Council; George Hicks, secretary of the Amalgamated Union of Building Trades Workers and A. W. Haycock, M.P.[4]

But aside from these labor sources, of which only a few have been quoted, there are many others. A group of British investigators, headed by E. P. Tetsall, chairman of Messrs. William Brown of Ipswich, and made up of prominent English business men, including W. O. Woodward, and William Thompson, visited Leningrad, Kem, Soroka, Onega, Keret and Archangel in 1931. They reported that they were unable to find the slightest signs of forced labor. On the contrary, "The workmen are in excellent condition, look cheerful and contented," they reported.

"Our independent inquiries and observations convince us that the labor conditions are excellent and that the rates of remuneration agreed with the unions are satisfactory to the workmen. We saw Red Cross huts, rest rooms and large dining rooms, also many more buildings in the course of erection. The most careful inquiries fail to disclose anything in the nature of forced labor now or at any time," reads their report. After a tour of the Archangel lumber centers, the delegation reported that "there is not a scrap of evidence that forced labor ever existed." It further stated that the people were found well nourished, clean and happy. Workers loading ships are paid at a double rate for overtime. The committee particularly noticed the care given children and their happy appearance and the cleanliness of nurseries and schools. Workers' clubs and the cheerful and eager demeanor of the young people also impressed them forcibly.[5]

AMERICANS ALSO DENY FORCED LABOR CHARGES

Many American authorities who visited the Soviet Union have reported that there is no forced labor in the timber industry. Representative Henry T. Rainey of Illinois, majority leader in the House of Representatives, who visited the Soviet Union in 1931, declared in an interview:

I particularly investigated the question of forced labor in Russia and there isn't any there. Labor is freer in Russia than in any country in the world. There is one disadvantage under which Russia now operates—that the workers have more money than ever before, and they are spending it liberally in travelling, literally by tens of thousands of people, from one job to another. They are sure of their employment wherever they stop, and they can go back to their original employment any time.[6]

H. R. Knickerbocker, correspondent of the New York *Evening Post,* in a speech over the Columbia Broadcasting system, June 21, 1931, said:

I worked as correspondent in Moscow for two years and last year I travelled about 10,000 miles through the Soviet Union to make a report on the Five-Year Plan for the New York *Evening Post* and the Philadelphia *Public Ledger.* If the Russian people are in chains, they have put them on since I was there.

Walter Duranty, who has lived in Russia for 10 years as the correspondent of the New York *Times,* writing about labor discipline and the tendency of workers to criticize orders given by technical superiors instead of carrying them out, said: "This contrasts somewhat curiously with talk abroad about 'forced labor' in Soviet factories and anthracite fields. . . . In your correspondent's opinion . . . as an American expressed it . . . 'labor here is too darned free and too darned talkative'." [7]

Testifying before the Ways and Means Committee of the House of Representatives, January 28, 1931, Colonel Hugh L. Cooper, noted American engineer and builder of the great Dnieprostroy power dam, stated that "in all the years I have spent in Russia, I have never seen convicts employed in any way with production." At another time he declared "investigations were carried out by some of the leading business men of this country. They have now put themselves on record refuting the forced labor allegations."

None of these reports seems to be as exhaustive as the series of articles by Henry Wales of the Chicago *Tribune* which was also carried in the New York *Times,* beginning March 27, 1931:

I have just completed a fortnight's investigation of labor conditions in the North district and inspection of logging camps along the Dvina and Pinega rivers, and am the first foreign correspondent to visit this region since the wholesale exile of kulaks (rich peasants) into this zone last year. . . .

My investigation covered three phases—first, convict labor; second, forced labor and, third, the living conditions of the kulaks and native workers here.

The initial question can be disposed of at once. Convict labor is not employed by the State Timber Trust for export production.

The question of compulsory labor opens various aspects and no definite conclusion can be drawn without defining more clearly the exact terms. All the inhabitants of the region, native populace as well as the exiles, are forced to work to make a living—they must labor to exist.

But, technically speaking, they are not forced to perform any specific kind of labor—they are not drafted by the State Timber Trust or required to execute any given task. . . .

In the forest near Orletzy I visited a camp where thirty-five expert Norwegian lumberjacks had been imported to teach the most efficient methods. The Norwegians use the model ribbon saw and the American style narrow-blade axe. They told me they had just renewed their contract to remain two years more in the Russian forests and that they had no complaints to make with living or working conditions. . . .

Everywhere I was impressed by the scarcity of soldiers—the militia, as the local police and members of the GPU are called . . . Despite their arduous labor, the girls manage to keep themselves looking well, preserving their hands with woolen mittens and leather gloves. And they do not need lipstick or rouge to give them the rosiest of complexions.

In the same series Wales quotes Michael Tzetlin, Vice-Chairman of the executive committee of the Archangel Soviet, as saying:

The state is helping them [the kulaks] to build homes and create new villages, composed of kulaks exclusively, where they can hunt, fish, farm, enter the timber industry or do whatever they please. The government is giving them all the land they want, providing lumber, building materials, food supplies and clothing and establishing postal, telegraph and transportation services in the newly opened territory.

Other work being offered the kulaks includes railroad and highway construction, draining swampy tundra and reclaiming rich farming land. They are not guarded in any way. Their death rate is not above the local rate. Intermarriage with local inhabitants is common.

On the invitation of the Soviet timber exporting company, two Americans, Spencer Williams, Moscow representative of the American-Russian Chamber of Commerce, and Myron G. Doll, American engineer, accompanied by Robin Kinkead, New York *Times* correspondent, spent a part of June, 1932, visiting the timber country in the Archangel district and the northern Dvina River. They afterwards made affidavits as to what they saw.

In Archangel the party visited sawmills and lumber yards and watched the loading of ships, and in no case could they find anything that looked like forced or convict labor. The visitors talked directly with scores of workers—without the use of an interpreter—and the workers were unanimous in agreeing that they were working of their own free will and could leave whenever they liked. According to their affidavits the young workers engaged in this work hooted any suggestion that they were working against their will. They said: "In Soviet Russia every one must work if he wants to earn a living—that is the only forced thing about our labor." [8]

LABOR TURNOVER AND THE LABOR CODE

The high labor turnover in the Soviet Union also contradicts the charges of "forced labor." Joseph Freeman points out in *The Soviet Worker* that,

As a matter of simple logic, it is difficult to reconcile "armed guards" with an absenteeism so great that it endangers the "execution of the year's plan." The tremendous labor turnover in Soviet industry—about 150 per cent a year—would seem in itself to be a refutation of the "forced labor" charges. It is impossible for labor to be "conscripted" and yet to move from job to job at so rapid a rate. The fact is that the special inter-

ests which circulate "forced labor" charges make little effort to be either accurate or consistent (our emphasis).[9]

Furthermore, the very existence of the Soviet Labor Code explodes the false charges of "forced labor" in the Soviet Union. As Freeman points out, "The Labor Code guarantees the freedom of labor by protecting the worker against dismissal without valid cause; by granting him the right to break an agreement concluded for an indefinite period regardless of whether he has valid cause or not; and the right to break a labor agreement without notice in case the employer violates the conditions of the agreement or the labor laws. Under such circumstances, where the worker has freedom of contract, 'forced labor' is impossible."

In addition to the Labor Code, however, the labor agreements with the trade unions, safety rules and social insurance give the Soviet worker a degree of protection unequaled anywhere in the world.

There is, however, one section of the Soviet Labor Code, which has been variously misunderstood or willfully misrepresented by Soviet enemies as requiring forced labor. The provision is explained by Freeman:

"Under Soviet law there exists a type of obligatory labor in cases of emergency common in other countries. Paragraph 11 of the Labor Code provides that under extraordinary circumstances involving natural calamities, such as fighting the elements, or in case of a shortage of labor for the fulfillment of the most important state requirements, citizens may be called upon to perform obligatory labor."

Thus in such regions as Central Asia and Transcaucasia, where the welfare and safety of the community depend on keeping the canals in good repair or the building of new ones, such decrees are in effect. And since the community as a whole undertakes to keep the irrigation works in proper shape, the individual peasant is obliged to contribute his labor to that end. Those sharing in the benefits of the irrigation systems who live too far away to work at the communal tasks contribute in the form of a tax.

The Labor Code provision with regard to obligatory work in case of labor shortage is resorted to only on the rare occasions of extreme emergency—a life and death matter—in which some particular kind of work is indispensable to the national safety. Emergencies of this kind occurred in 1931 when an acute need arose for specialists and technicians in railway and water transportation, and similarly, in connection with the spring sowing campaign of the same year when there was an urgent need of agricultural experts and technicians.

The mobilization of the transportation experts was carried on among those formerly engaged in this type of work whose skill was needed in the emergency. It did not apply to those already employed in the field. In many cases these experts were given higher wages in accord with the greater degree of skill required for their tasks. The agricultural experts were paid all traveling expenses and continued to receive their salaries from the institutions which employed them and to which they returned at the end of two months.

In no case, however, does this mobilization imply the use of force or compulsion. The worst that may befall one refusing such work is the loss of the job held at the time, in which case he may earn a living at unskilled labor. *He cannot, however, be forced to accept work which he does not desire.* With the present acute shortage of labor, being struck off the labor exchange list can scarcely be called a grave penalty.

More About Soviet Timber

Most of the charges of "forced labor" in the Soviet Union, as we have noted, have centered on the northern timber industry. Such charges do not bear up under examination. In the first place it must be understood that lumbering, even in the most highly industrialized countries and under the very best of conditions, is no picnic. In no country have timber cutting conditions been worse than in the United States. Indeed, they are so bad in this country that only the hardiest men can stand the work. The writer has visited many timber camps and company lumber towns in East Texas where conditions of virtual peonage exist. Fortunes piled up by such companies as the Kirby Lumber Co. and the Great Southern Lumber Co. were made by vicious exploitation of timber workers. Taking the facts about timber production internationally into consideration, Soviet timber conditions show up well in comparison.

In old Russia as well as in the Soviet Union timber work has always been a seasonal industry. It has always been performed largely by peasants during the winter season and has always supplied part of their income.

About 54% of all the seasonal workers throughout the tsarist empire were too poor to pay traveling expenses and were, therefore, obliged to walk long distances from their homes to find employment. It has been estimated that 12,500,000 workdays were wasted every year by these enforced treks.

A lack of labor legislation under the old régime left the peasant seasonal worker completely unprotected. He obtained employment either by selling his labor power directly to an employer or by becoming a member of a group hired by a contractor. No laws regulated the number of hours, wages, hiring or firing, general working conditions or sanitation. As a result even tsarist government reports reveal grave abuses.

Until the October Revolution the working conditions in the Russian timber camps were as bad as anywhere in the world. The men worked from 10 to 11 and frequently 12 hours a day. At present Soviet lumbermen, like other Soviet workers, put in a little over seven hours a day. Since the Revolution such conveniences as baths, laundries, first aid stations, drug stores and, in some cases, even dental laboratories have appeared in the woods. To-day there are facilities for recreation and education—newspapers, books, writing material, radios, sports, movies and dances.

An interesting and informative article by A. L. Gorsky on Soviet timber conditions appeared in the May, 1932, issue of the *British Russian Gazette and Trade Outlook.* It said in part:

> Under the Five-Year Plan now nearing fulfillment, no less than 35,000,000 rubles will have been spent on the provision of dwellings for the workers in newly-developed or uninhabited forest regions. In these dwellings provision is made for clubs, study circles, baths and drying rooms, whilst medical assistance, and such amenities as it is possible to provide in isolated regions, are also placed at the workers' disposal.
>
> In the single financial year 1930-31 the huge sum of 29,500,000 rubles was spent on social insurance for the timber industry alone. This insurance provides for the workers during temporary disablement of themselves or their dependents, and includes free medical attention. They are provided for with bonuses to cover the expenses of the birth and rearing of their children through various stages of life to funeral expenses and pensions for their dependent relatives on the death of the wage earner.

The article reports that direct wages have increased in the last few years by 35.8% for sawmillers, 50% for lumbermen and rafters, and 26% for transport workers in the forests, while the cost of most articles of consumption is gradually being lowered.

THE KULAKS AND FORCED LABOR

It is important to note that the campaign against "forced labor" in the Soviet Union reached its height at the time when the movement for collectivization in Soviet agriculture had gained great momentum and the kulaks were being "liquidated as a class." It was natural that the class of well-to-do village sharks, remnant of capitalism in a society building socialism, should have the sympathies of the capitalists abroad. Accordingly, many of the charges of "forced labor" in the U.S.S.R. were linked up with the charge that the kulaks were being "liquidated" (eliminated) by harnessing them in forced labor under conditions calculated to wipe them out. Of course, it was not a question of actually "liquidating" the kulaks by physical extermination, but *as a class, i.e.,* by changing the economic organization of agriculture in such a way as to make impossible the existence of a class of rich peasants who live by exploiting the poor peasants. Capitalist propagandists, however, deliberately distorted the facts and with the aid of white guard émigrés, socialists, Mensheviks and lie-manufacturing centers in the Baltic countries, spread stories of the killing off of the kulaks. The great majority of the kulaks who were expelled from the collectivized regions by vote of the members of the community migrated to other districts where they either settled on the land or obtained jobs as artisans or laborers.

There are no concentration camps and no forced labor for kulaks or former kulaks as charged by the capitalist propagandists, nor are there special laws against kulaks who commit crimes in violation of the penal code, such as murder or arson. After conviction such a person is a prisoner on the same basis and has the same status as an industrial worker who is a prisoner.

THE STATUS OF SOVIET CONVICT LABOR

The actual status of convict labor in the Soviet Union makes a significant contrast to that of convict labor in the United States. Penal methods in the Soviet Union are entirely different from those in any other country in the world. There is no thought of degrading and breaking the spirit of the prisoners in the Soviet Union. Prisoners are treated as diseased persons or as victims of circumstances. Every effort is made to rehabilitate the criminal by proper medical and social treatment. The brutal slave-driving conditions under which convicts work in the United States are, therefore, impossible in the Soviet Union. Every prison there has a staff of trained physicians and psychiatrists who examine and treat prisoners; schools where the prisoners are given the elements of education; and workshops where they are taught useful trades. No prisoner leaves illiterate or without a real vocation. Work in prisons is not designed to punish the prisoner or to humiliate him. Its aim is entirely educational.

Prisoners are usually sent to Labor Communes, where they live in healthful surroundings. Cultural pursuits are encouraged. For instance in Commune No. 2 the members have organized cultural circles, orchestras, dramatic groups, literary groups, lectures, radio clubs, sports, a summer theater and physical training groups. In Commune No. 3 more than 54% of the inmates had no professional training before their commitment for theft. Yet in four years 163 of them completely broke with their old habits, were accepted in labor unions and their criminal records erased.

Maxim Gorky in describing a celebration at a prison commune where 25 young men received prizes in recognition of their work, where 36 were given back their civil rights, and 74 given union cards, said: "I sat in the presidium and saw that among these 1,500 people many also were near tears—tears of joy for their comrades. They had been resurrected to a new life, people who before the October Revolution would never have known resurrection—never."

Major C. E. Lovejoy, executive secretary of the Alumni Federation of Columbia University, told of conditions in Soviet prisons in an interview with the New York *Times*, August 22, 1931. Major Lovejoy had just returned from a tour of the Soviet Union as leader of a group traveling under the auspices of the American Institute of Educational Travel. He said:

What amazed me most is the system of rehabilitation of the prisoners. There is a school in the prison and each prisoner is trained for some profession, so that when he is liberated he will not be tempted by want to commit crimes again.

The prison cells, according to Mr. Lovejoy, are open from 5 A.M. until 10 P.M. and each inmate is virtually his own "trusty," allowed to come and go as he pleases within the confines of the prison. The atmosphere of the place is rather jovial, the prisoners seemingly being quite contented with their lot. A radio was found in every cell. The visitors were surprised to learn that prisoners were given two weeks vacation annually and allowed to go home during that time.

In the Soviet Union every effort is made to solve the sex problem of prisoners which is permitted to degrade prison life under capitalism, causing widespread homosexuality in every large American prison. While visiting the Lefortovo Prison at Moscow a *United Press* correspondent found that "men and women convicts respectively are allowed to spend week-ends with their husbands and wives in special cells belonging to the prison." [10]

Roger N. Baldwin, director of the American Civil Liberties Union, after a thorough study of the prison labor problem in the Soviet Union, reported:

One of the great improvements in Russian prisons is that work is available to almost all prisoners. There is no forced labor, no contract labor, as in the United States. All prisoners are free not to work if they choose. But great inducements to work lie in the payment of wages and in the deduction of one-third time off the sentences of working prisoners.[11]

Walter Duranty substantiates the above statements:

. . . in view of the possible discussion of the subject in the United States or elsewhere, your correspondent would like to put the following statement on record:

Criminals, in the ordinary sense of the word, are better treated in the Soviet Union than in any other country—with due allowance for universal shortage of living quarters and commodities. They work, but they get trade union rates for their labor, the produce of which is sold exclusively within the Soviet Union, and they have "parole" holidays yearly, which they almost never break.[12]

All these experts bear out what Soviet officials themselves say about the condition of prisoners in the Soviet Union. They have never denied that prisoners are used in public works such as roads and railroad construction and other such work, as well as in manufacturing certain articles none of which are exported.

Socialist Labor vs. Capitalist Labor

In the first chapter of this book we analyzed labor under capitalism and found all wage labor to be forced labor, either indirect forced labor, caused by the whip of starvation wielded by the capitalists who own the land and means of production, or direct forced labor where open physical or legal restraint is used.

In the U.S.S.R., the working class owns all the means of production; it is working for its own benefit and is building Socialism. Hence, in the U.S.S.R., labor is really free. Workers in a socialist society are free, for they are not oppressed by a ruling class. Marx and Lenin have shown that any other sort of freedom is a mockery and a sham. Referring to labor in the Soviet Union, Lenin wrote:

> For the first time, after centuries of compulsory toil for the benefit of others, of labor under subjection for the benefit of the exploiters, it becomes possible for the workers to work for their own benefit, to work on the basis of all the latest achievements of technology and culture.

The defenders of capitalism may dispute this and contend that in the U.S.S.R. the constraint to labor also is present, that is to say, the constraint of hunger, for if a worker does not work he will starve. In the U.S.S.R., they say, the workers also produce surplus value, for which they are not directly paid in the form of wages. What then is the difference between capitalism and the Soviet system of economy?

Our reply to the first point is that not only individual workers, but the whole working class of the Soviet Union would die of hunger if it did not work to produce the necessaries of life. We must draw a distinction between labor called forth by the natural need to satisfy human requirements, and labor forced by a hunger which is deliberately created under capitalism by one section of society, the ruling class, which monopolizes the means of production for the purpose of compelling the hungry producers to work for the benefit of the owning class. The fact that the producers, the workers, are deprived of the means of production, creating the whiplash of hunger, lies at the very basis of capitalism. In the Soviet system of economy there can be no hunger in this sense, as under this system all the means of production belong to the producers themselves. Here the stimulus to labor is to produce goods for the satisfaction of human needs and not for the profits of an exploiting class.

Free labor in a socialist society does not mean that members of that society may work, or refuse to work, just as they see fit. Socialist society is not a society of laggards or slackers. It is based rather on the labor of all members of society—with the exception of children, the aged, the infirm, the sick.

Under the Socialist economy of the Soviet Union, that portion of the total labor product which does not go directly to the Soviet worker for his personal consumption, is applied to the program for the economic betterment of the *whole social order*—thus accruing to the benefit of the working class as a whole—and not, as in capitalist society, to the support of a parasitic class of non-producers. The capital accumulation derived from the total labor product is thus applied to the improvement of the economic and cultural status of the working class.

As for "surplus value" this point is made clear by Joseph Freeman when he says:

. . . Soviet economists emphasize that one basic difference between the capitalist and socialist forms of economy lies in the re-distribution of capital accumulation. "Surplus value," in the sense in which it exists in the capitalist economy, does not exist in Soviet economy, since the latter eliminates private profit. Accordingly, while the individual worker forgoes part of the product of his labor so that basic capital may be accumulated, all such capital is spent in ways which accrue to the benefit of the working class as a whole, and none of it goes in the form of profits to unproductive groups of the population.

Moreover, it has never been maintained by Communists that in a socialist economy the worker receives for his own individual consumption the full product of his labor. The 13th congress of the Russian Communist Party in April, 1923, in discussing the problem of accumulating basic capital, stated that "only that industry can be victorious which gives more than it absorbs. Industry which exists at the expense of the budget . . . cannot create a stable and lasting support for the proletarian dictatorship. . . . The state trusts and combines have as their basic problem the securing of surplus value for the purpose of state accumulation, which alone can guarantee the raising of the material level of the country and a socialist reconstruction of the whole national economy."

In his *Criticism of the Gotha Program*, Karl Marx exploded the theory that in a socialist society the worker receives as his individual allotment the full product of his labor for his personal consumption. Marx pointed out that of the total social product of labor only a portion is distributed among individual producers of society for personal consumption; a considerable part of the labor product goes to satisfy the "economically necessary" needs of society, which are listed by Marx as "First, the amount required for the replacement of the means of production used up. Secondly, an additional portion for the expansion of production. Thirdly, a reserve and insurance fund against mischance, disturbances through forces of nature, etc."

In addition to the foregoing "economically necessary" deductions from the total product of labor, Marx lists an additional group of deductions which might be termed "socially necessary": "First, the general administrative expenses that do not form a part of production. . . . Secondly, that portion which is destined for the satisfaction of common wants, such as schools, provision for the protection of the public health, etc. . . . Thirdly, funds for those unable to work, etc., in short, for what now belongs to so-called public charity."

Only after these deductions—the "economically necessary" and the "socially necessary"—are made from the total product of labor do we finally have that part of the consumption fund which is distributed among the individual producers.

The tasks confronting the Russian working class, which owns the industries of the country and holds political power, are thus entirely different from those which confront the workers in other countries who are oppressed and exploited by the capitalists. The working class, as the owner of the means of production, besides striving to improve its own conditions of life and labor, must also strive to develop socialist production to the utmost, to construct giant works according to the latest technical achievements, to strengthen the state and to raise the whole cultural level of the population. For this purpose the working class has to create a social reserve; it must secure means with which to make improvements in machinery and science and to replace worn-out production goods. Does the creation of these reserve funds mean that the working class is exploited? Certainly not. The working class creates these funds not for an exploiting class but for itself. Marx, in his *Criticism of the Gotha Program,* emphasized this when he wrote: "That which the producer loses as a private individual comes back to him in the form of direct or indirect benefits as a member of society." Obviously under such circumstances there can be no exploitation of the worker; there can be no forced labor.

STIMULI FOR INCREASING PRODUCTION

Even the enemies of the Soviet Union concede that tremendous results are being achieved in developing the industries and agriculture of the country. Even they are forced to admit that the first Five-Year Plan is being successfully completed. If it is not forced labor which furnishes the incentive for such accomplishments, then what are the incentives? There are two main motives which make the Soviet worker strive to increase production. The first is class stimulus—the desire to advance the cause of the working class both in the Soviet Union and in the entire world. This feeling was expressed recently by Joseph Stalin, secretary of the Communist Party of the Soviet Union. He said:

We must advance so that the working class of the whole world, seeing us, may say: "There is our vanguard, there is our shock brigade, there is the workers' fatherland—they are working for their cause, our cause; good, we shall support them against the capitalists and advance the world revolution." Shall we justify the hopes of the working class of the world? Yes, we must, if we do not want to disgrace ourselves in the end.

The second motive is the desire for personal, material and cultural gain as well as the desire to receive recognition of personal worth as a contributor to society. This personal gain includes higher wages, shorter hours, social insurance, education, recreation and the reward of honor which comes with labor well-performed and not at the expense of others. In the capitalist world the thing most desired is to get money and become a parasite, to live on interest, not to have to work. In the Soviet Union work is the thing which receives social approbation. The shock-brigader in industry becomes the hero of labor and he is highly esteemed by his fellow workers.

The wage worker under capitalism on the other hand is not interested in increasing production. He gets no social prestige thereby, as manual labor especially is regarded as degrading and is not done by the "best" people. Nor does he receive material benefits by increasing production. To increase the productivity of labor under capitalism means lower wages and a larger army of unemployed. The worker is not interested in technical improvements, for all means of production under capitalism are at the same time means of exploitation; technical improvements only increase unemployment. The worker is not interested in lowering the cost of production which brings gain only to the capitalist. The worker knows that the sapping of his health and the reduction of his standard of living are only means of increasing the rate of profit for the capitalists. Consequently the only stimulus to labor for him is the whip of hunger, the fear of being dismissed, or the policeman's club when on strike.

SOCIALIST COMPETITION AND SHOCK BRIGADES

A new spirit is already evidenced in the Soviet Union in what has become known as "socialist competition." Under socialist competition a group of workers in a certain factory competes with another group in the same factory to see which can do its job most quickly and in the most efficient manner. Or workers of an entire factory challenge and compete with the workers of another factory, mine or farm.

It sometimes happens that a factory or an industry falls behind in its allotted task under the plan because of a temporary lack of transportation facilities or for some other reason. To meet such emergencies "shock brigades" have been organized. These are groups of enthusiastic workers that volunteer to help overcome the obstacles in the lagging factory. When it has finished its job the brigade transfers its efforts to another emergency. Gay celebrations follow victorious completion of a particular job. Shock brigaders are rewarded accordingly and are given prizes among which the most treasured is the medal of the Order of Lenin.

To-day socialist competition has become the driving force in the carrying out of the Five-Year Plans. At the beginning of 1931 there were 2,500,000 workers organized into shock brigades. Besides these two methods of increasing production there are other methods of competition and emulation. Thus as Stalin said, "Labor, from being the shameful, heavy burden it was considered to be in the past, becomes a cause of honor, of glory, of gallantry, and of heroism." The Five-Year Plans are not being achieved by the fear of loss of job or any other capitalist coercion, but by the enthusiasm, the creative activity and class-conscious discipline of the broad masses of workers.

For over a century bourgeois economists have argued that socialism was impossible because, they contended, in a socialist society there would be no incentive for further development. Everything would remain at a standstill. There would be no motive for work. Their stock answer was "competition is the life blood of trade." The capitalists and their agents simply cannot "imagine" labor other than that produced by fear of starvation or some other form of coercion.

Therefore, when the capitalists are forced to acknowledge the tremendous progress in the Soviet Union they shout that it is only possible to have such development under some system of coerced or involuntary labor. It is evident, furthermore, that the Soviet workers are not starving else they could not have accomplished such an enormous amount of work. Accordingly the capitalists and their agents attempt to dispel the favorable impression the Soviet form of labor might make on their own forced laborers by raising the cry of "forced labor" in the U.S.S.R. They contend that "free" workers under capitalism cannot compete with "forced labor" under socialism.

The Soviet workers and peasants have proved to the whole world that the capitalists and their apologists are wrong, that the workers' society does develop science and invention, that the masses are able to manage the industries and the farms. While the capitalist world is hopelessly stuck in the mud of an international crisis, the Soviet Union has no unemployment and marches ahead. In the space of a few years they are transforming a backward agricultural country into a highly developed industrial country. The dictatorship of the proletariat is releasing the creative energy of millions of workers and peasants.

This creative energy of the masses is expressed especially by the shock brigaders and other workers engaged in socialist competition. The record of achievements in the building of Soviet industry and in the reorganization of agriculture abounds with hundreds of cases of real labor heroism by shock brigades whose example inspired the masses of workers to greater enthusiasm and made possible the completion of the Five-Year Plan in four years. Enthusiastic oil workers brought about the completion of the Five-Year Plan in that industry in two and a half years. The workers of numerous factories, such as the Moscow Brake Works, the Kolomensk and Kharkov locomotive plants and the Moscow Electric Works, also completed the first Five-Year Plan for their factories in two and a half years.

And when the Soviet workers overtake and surpass the advanced industrial capitalist nations, the wealth and power of the workers will be higher than any ever known in the history of the world. This will be a glaring contrast to what happens when one capitalist country surpasses another capitalist country, which is done only by more intensive exploitation of the workers, longer hours, lower wages and poor conditions of work.

The more class-conscious workers and more advanced peasants are in the Communist Party and in the Young Communist League (Komsomol), which are the center of organization and inspiration in carrying out the work of building socialism. Komsomols especially play a decisive rôle in overcoming the anti-social habits inherited by the workers from capitalism and replacing them by a realization of the great historical task which has fallen to the working class of the Soviet Union. A free working class, conscious of its freedom and its rôle, has shown in the Soviet Union how limitless are its energies.

Soviet Labor Unions

Strong labor unions safeguard workers' conditions in the U.S.S.R. There are now (1932) nearly 17 million trade union members. The American Federation of Labor in contrast has less than 2,500,000 actual members in good standing.

But the officials of the A. F. of L. still contend that the Soviet trade unions are not "free." What they mean is that they don't support Democrats in one town and Republicans in another; they are not "business unions" and rackets; they don't subscribe to life insurance sold by Matthew Woll; they are not dictated to by the employers' National Civic Federation and the American Legion fascists. They don't assist a capitalist government in preparing for imperialist wars for plunder, as does the A. F. of L.

There is plenty of testimony, even from bourgeois sources, as to the freedom and strength of the Soviet trade unions. For instance, Sherwood Eddy, who has made six visits to the U.S.S.R., says in his book, *The Challenge of Russia:*

There is a healthy trade union democracy among the workers. Economically free, independent of any individual employers, apprehensive of no arbitrary discharge or neglected employment, the laboring class at least is encouraged in the freedom of expression and the right of criticism of industry or the government.

Another observer, Dr. George M. Price, director of the Joint Board of Sanitary Control of New York, and an authority on factory inspection in the garment industry, referring to the part played by the trade unions in the Soviet Union, said:

The principal function of the unions and their representatives in the provincial district councils as well as within the establishment itself is the protection of the individual workers in their economic, political and other rights.

All wage contracts, individual and collective agreements are made through the Factory Committee and through the organs of the unions, which see to it that the worker is placed in as high a wage rank as possible, and as he is entitled to.

The union also protects the worker in all matters of dispute, conflict, and questions of right of discharge, which may come up during employment. The union through its organs, and especially through its social insurance activities, takes care of the workers during sickness, unemployment, invalidity, or in case of death. . . .[13]

HOURS, WAGES AND SOCIAL INSURANCE

Both money or nominal wages and real wages have been increasing steadily in the Soviet Union. By the fiscal year 1928-29 nominal wages were 190% and real wages 43% higher than in 1913. In 1930 the annual wages of all workers showed a gain of 12.6% over the preceding year, and in 1931 there was a further gain of 23.5%. The greatest gains in wages were in heavy industry where the wages had been the lowest before the Revolution.

During the period of the Five-Year Plan, increase in wages kept pace with the rapid increase in production. Thus the average annual wages of workers in census industry increased from 778 rubles in the fiscal year 1926-27 to 1,167 rubles in 1931, *a gain of 50 per cent.*[14]

Only recently there was a still further increase. The New York *Times,* April 1, 1932, reported, "The industrial pay rises are designed to keep pace with demands made upon the workers by the scheduled increase of 36% in industrial production." Thus along with increases in production go increases in pay. This is in marked contrast to decreases in pay with increases in production in capitalist countries.

But cash wages for work are only a part of the total wages. If indirect payments received by the Soviet worker are taken into account—such as social insurance benefits, free medical aid, vacations with pay, low or free rent, free working clothes, cultural facilities, etc.,—wages are increased by an average of from 20 to 35%. If these indirect payments are included, real wages at the end of 1931 may be estimated at about double the pre-war figure.[15]

Before we consider the Soviet benefits from social insurance and other privileges let us compare working hours of tsarist Russia in 1913 with those of the Soviet Union in 1931. Tsarist work days averaged around 10 hours, although workers often toiled 10 to 16 hours a day. It was only after the October Revolution that the 8-hour day became, both in law and in practice, the maximum for the adult population and the 6-hour day the maximum for minors up to the age of 18 and all workers in hazardous occupations. Children under 16 are forbidden to work except in certain instances when necessary for their training or education, in which case children over 14 may work 4 hours a day. Over 70% of the workers in large-scale industry are on the 7-hour day, and by the end of 1932 it was planned to have 92% on this basis. By the end of the second Five-Year Plan the 6-hour day is expected to be universal within the borders of the Soviet Union.

Social insurance has been developed further in the Soviet Union than in any country in the world. All workers are insured from the very first day of their work, and have full rights to all the benefits. The worker pays nothing whatever for the insurance and all the expense is paid by the employers.

A worker and his family are entitled to receive full medical aid, *i.e.,* free medicine, doctor's care, sanitariums and treatment, in addition to cash pay. An American friend of the author, a former Georgia cotton mill worker, writes from Kharkov where her husband is a mechanic, that she has been getting the care of a specialist and free electric treatments for a small growth on her neck. She says, "such care, even if I could have afforded it at all in the United States, would have cost a fortune." She probably contracted the trouble while working as a child laborer in a Georgia mill—where she started work at eight years of age. Now she is being cured free of charge in the Soviet Union!

During temporary disability due to sickness, accident, or any other cause, the worker gets help to the amount of 75 to 100% of his regular wages. A pregnant woman is freed from work eight weeks before and eight weeks after childbirth. Women and men workers receive equal pay for equal work. All expenses connected with the birth of a child are covered for the worker-mother. Then for nine months there is an allowance for milk. Funeral expenses for a worker or any members of his family are also paid.

Unemployment relief was given while some unemployment still prevailed in the Soviet Union. But to-day, as has been said, there is no unemployment and, therefore, no need for relief.

Pensioners are paid in case of complete disability from industrial accident or occupational disease. In fixing the pension the length of time the worker was employed is not considered. There is also an old age pension which begins at the age of 60 for men, 55 for women and 50 for miners. It amounts to as much as 55% of total earnings.

Safety and sanitation are stressed throughout the Soviet industrial system. In building factories special attention is given to comfort and health—proper lighting, ventilation, safety devices and sanitation. As a result the rate of fatal accidents in 1929 was lower than in Germany or the United States.

EDUCATION AND CULTURE

Education is another field where the workers in the Soviet Union have made remarkable progress. The years 1930-31 marked a big step toward the goal of universal elementary education. The total number of pupils in the elementary and secondary schools in 1930-31 amounted to 19.3 millions, as compared with 7.8 millions in 1914 and 11.9 millions in

1929. During the past few years the development of the network of trade and technical schools has advanced at a rate even more rapid than that of general schools.

In 1914 there were 109,000 students in the higher institutions of learning. By 1931 this number had more than trebled. Students in the technical and factory schools—exclusive of vocational schools, vocational workshops and the like—totaled 1,808,000 in 1931, or practically seven times the pre-war figure. In addition, several million workers and collective farmers are extending their education by evening schools, correspondence courses, and by other means. In 1931 the Soviet government spent seven and a half times as much for education as was spent in 1914 under the Tsar.

Workers are favored in many other ways. Frequently free tickets are given to theaters, movies, and other entertainments. Then there are clubs in every factory with libraries, gymnasiums and rest rooms. Some of the finest buildings in the entire country have been converted into club buildings. The workers also get the best food and housing obtainable.

Workers in the Soviet Union enjoy the best of everything available. Instead of the Vanderbilts and the Romanovs it is the workers who are the privileged. All of this is in glaring contrast to the situation in a capitalist country where a rich minority own the entire country and are able to enjoy all the material advantages of life while hundreds of thousands starve or go undernourished for lack of bread.

General William N. Haskell, chief of the American Relief Administration in Russia in 1921-23, who recently returned from the Soviet Union, declares that what the worker gets that makes him better off than any other class, and more satisfied, is his feeling of importance in the socialistic order. He is the element most favored by the government, and his voice is the controlling factor in industry and politics. Thus, "today, the worker has a feeling that he counts—and a vast hope for the future. In tsarist days he had nothing." [16]

The Russian workers had to overcome many obstacles to advance as far as they have. After the Revolution they came into possession of a war-ravaged country. Then followed violent counter-revolution, led by the capitalists and monarchists, backed by the armies of England, Japan, France, the United States and other countries. Military intervention failed but the capitalist nations continued to boycott the young Soviet Republic. Credit could not be obtained to rebuild what had been destroyed by war and famine. Backward methods of production had been inherited from the old régime. Factories were idle or entirely out of commission.

But though the capitalists of the world have vainly tried by war, blockade and lies to prevent the success of the Soviet Union the workers in other countries have helped it. Not only have they blocked war plots against the Soviets but many thousands of workers from almost every country are in the factories and on the farms of the Soviet Union helping to build socialism. They write with glowing enthusiasm of what they find there.

In January, 1931, a group of American workers in Stalingrad wrote:

We, a group of American technicians employed at the Stalingrad Tractor Plant, take exception to the misleading propaganda that is aiming to influence the minds of the peoples of the foreign countries toward the Soviet Union.

Having been afforded the opportunity of living and working in the U.S.S.R. during the epoch-making period . . . we have witnessed the initial efforts of the people in their industrial program, which, minus the prevailing enthusiasm of the masses, would be impossible of accomplishment.

It is such groups of workers, together with the hundreds of thousands of workers and sympathizers in other lands, who now form the real friends of the Soviet Union. It is they who from their own experience as workers must answer directly and sharply the stream of lies about "forced labor" in the only land where labor is really free.

CHAPTER X

SUMMARY AND CONCLUSION

F ROM the slavery of the time of the Egyptian Pharaohs to present-day capitalism the history of labor is the history of forced labor. Under slave systems, under feudalism and to-day under capitalism all labor necessary for the life of society has been carried out by an oppressed class, which has been deprived of most of the good things of life created by it and given only enough to assure its procreation and life from one day of toil to the next. The various systems of labor exploitation have differed only in the methods employed by the ruling class to force the workers to labor.

Under a pre-capitalist form of labor, the exploiters use direct force for extracting forced labor: the exploited are deprived of personal liberty; serfs are bound to the land of a manorial lord; compulsory labor laws are passed, etc. This is direct forced labor. Under capitalism, as we have pointed out in Chapter I, the exploiters use indirect, hidden coercion to make the workers produce surplus value. Starvation is the principal method of compulsion, although more direct methods of physical force are used when the need arises.

Within the borders of the United States, as we have tried to show in this book, we find forced labor of the most direct type in connection with unemployment "relief" and various public and private "charitable" institutions. We find forced labor in prisons and on chain gangs. We find peonage widespread; and in the American colonies and semi-colonies we find every form of direct forced labor.

If the capitalists and their apologists really want to find convict labor they should begin their search at home and not in the Soviet Union, the only free labor country in the world.

As we have shown they would find in the United States that several hundred thousand prisoners in state, federal, city and county prisons are producing many millions of dollars worth of convict-made goods. These commodities are being sold in the general market, both at home and abroad, under the most despicable methods, furnishing cut-throat competition with "free" labor in a time of economic crisis when at least 16,000,000 "free" workers are jobless. They would find that the conditions under which these goods are produced are more horrible than those the most consummate liar among all the patrioteers and monarchists has been able to concoct about the Soviet Union. In the United States we find: women hung up on pegs like hams of meat; men confined in the stocks, in dungeons, in disease-infested holes on bread and water; men whipped to death and smothered in sweat boxes. In fact we find all the tortures used by the decadent ruling classes throughout history. All these tortures are administered for not doing enough work.

The prisoners who are thus exploited, victimized and murdered are workers. Most of them are guilty of "crimes" of hunger and unemployment, many are the victims of the third degree and the frame-up. Others are political prisoners who are imprisoned for their labor activities. The rich, controlling the courts and the law-making bodies, go free.

The prime motive of this system of convict labor is the desire for profit. This is true whether the convict works for a private employer or for the state. The Wickersham report on penal institutions was forced to admit that no wages, or at best in a few cases insignificant wages, are paid the convicts. There is no workmen's compensation, other than nominal compensation in only two states, for the prisoners who are forced to work under criminally dangerous conditions. The highest prison authorities are forced to admit that there is not a single well-rounded-out educational program for prison inmates in a single prison in the country. No real vocational training is given. Where is the vocational training in making a farmer push a needle or a city industrial worker a plow, or an office clerk a coal shovel? Why are workers driven to perform impossible tasks or suffer inhuman tortures? Is all this for reform?

Peonage is one of the most important types of forced labor in the United States, as it involves tens of thousands of industrial workers and tenant farmers, chiefly Negroes. It is especially prevalent in the South where it has been used since the Civil War as a partial substitute for chattel slavery. It is also found in other parts of the country, as for example among Mexicans in the Southwest and in beet fields in Colorado, Kansas, Michigan.

Contrary to popular opinion peonage is still legalized in several southern states through laws which penalize the breaking of a contract, vagrancy laws and emigrant agency laws. But peonage does not depend upon law alone but also on extra-legal methods including physical force and terrorism.

Though there is no way of determining the exact proportions of the problem, the hundreds of instances of exposures of peonage cases during the past few years, as well as many actual court prosecutions that were forced upon the Department of Justice, indicate that peonage involves tens of thousands of victims. The many revolts, usually called "race riots," against these conditions are also eloquent testimony as to its prevalence.

This country's record of exploitation of forced labor in the colonies differs only slightly in degree, if at all, from that of other imperialist nations. Herbert Hoover, one of our foremost "humanitarians," has been engaged in trafficking in colonial forced labor on a large scale.

It has been estimated that one-fifth of all imports into the United States, especially coffee, rubber, tobacco, sugar, spices, oils, fruits, are produced in whole or in part by direct forced labor. A part of these colonial forced labor goods are produced in the colonies dominated by foreign imperialists. But most of them are produced in United States colonies, semi-colonies, or "independent" countries where much American finance capital is invested, such as in the Caribbean islands, in Central America, in certain parts of South America, Hawaii, the Philippines, Liberia and other countries.

The historic methods by which forced laborers have been recruited in these places is by the expropriation of the best land by foreign and domestic landlords and capitalists. In this way small peasant proprietors, or natives who tilled common lands have been forced to seek work for employers in order to exist. To speed up this process special taxes have often been levied so that the natives were forced to seek work from exploiters to pay the taxes. Also native chiefs are bribed or compelled to furnish forced laborers.

The worst direct forced labor conditions have existed in Cuba, Guatemala, Liberia, Haiti, Venezuela and the Philippines. In the Philippines, for example, Robert W. Hart, surgeon of the United States Health Service, stationed in the islands for many years, estimated in 1926 that 20% of the total laboring population are held in "practical slavery."

A new form of labor was ushered in by the October, 1917, Revolution in Russia. The essence of the Revolution was the expropriation of the capitalists and of the large land-owners and the seizure of power by the proletariat and the poorest strata of the peasantry. The formerly exploited and oppressed classes became the new ruling class; the former exploiters were suppressed. Through the succeeding years of the Revolution the whole economic and social structure of Russia is becoming socialized. The last bulwark of entrenched capitalism is rapidly being overcome by the collectivization of agriculture which is making impossible the existence of the individual peasant proprietor. The Second Five-Year Plan lays down as a practical task the emergence of a classless society, ready technically and ideologically to begin the transformation to Communism.

The means of production and distribution in the Soviet Union are in the hands of the workers and the proletarian state. The greater part of agriculture is already organized on socialist lines in Soviet state and collective farms. The whole economy of the country has been reorganized and is a planned economy. This is possible only under a socialist system. A tremendous cultural change is taking place. The material and cultural conditions of the workers have been greatly improved. Cultural life in the rural districts is making tremendous strides and the proverbial backwardness of the village is being abolished. Does this not prove that the U.S.S.R. is, so far, the only land of free labor in the real sense of the word, the only land where the workers are masters of their own destiny?

However, the workers and peasants of the U.S.S.R. are not yet satisfied with the successes they have achieved. The rate of development of socialist construction must be increased still more, technology must be mastered, the banner of socialist competition must be raised still higher.

For the international capitalists to charge that Soviet economy is based on forced labor in the face of the above facts gives weight to the charges that those who are conducting the holy crusade against the "terrible" Bolsheviks are not horrified at the thought of real forced labor in their own country. On the contrary they have proven themselves utterly callous on that score. They are, in fact, keenly interested in "forced labor," merely as a pretext for shutting off Soviet-American trade, for crippling the Five-Year Plan, and for preparing sentiment for war against the U.S.S.R. in order —they claim—to free the poor "forced laborers" in that country and place them again under the wonderfully benign protection of a capitalist system!

This is not the first time in history that the exploiting class has tried to discredit a workers' government and destroy it. And this is not the first time that capitalists have used the pretext of wanting "to liberate the victims" of such a government, in order to prepare for its overthrow by drowning it in the blood of the working class.

The same thing happened during the reign of the Paris Commune in 1871, when for a brief time the workers of France held power. Thiers, leader of the French bourgeoisie, charged that the Commune was a tyranny and used that as a pretext for destroying it.

"Thiers," writes Karl Marx, "denounced it [the First International] as the despot of labor, pretending to be its liberator. ... He tells Paris that he was only anxious to free it from the hideous tyrants who oppress it."

Thus in 1871 the French bourgeoisie and foreign capitalists waged war against Red Paris under slogans similar to those now being used to prepare war against the Soviet Union. The bourgeoisie, in 1871, talked about the "despots of labor" in Red Paris. Now they talk about slaves and "forced labor" in Red Russia. The enemies of the worker then said that Red Paris was oppressed by tyrants. To-day the capitalists and their spokesmen say the Soviet workers are under the "bloody tyranny" of the omnipotent O.G.P.U.

The rich French parasites of 1871 posed as the emancipators of labor. The story of how they "freed" the workers of Paris can be read on the "Wall of the Communards" in the cemetery, *Père Lachaise*, in Paris. The Paris Commune, the first workers' government in history, was drowned in the blood of its heroic defenders. The workers of Paris were shackled again.

The international capitalists, including those of the United States, who exploit actual colonial slaves as well as forced labor in their own countries, would like to "emancipate" the Soviet "slaves" in the same way the Paris workers were "freed." Hence the campaign of hate and lies about forced labor in the Soviet Union. Hence the preparations for war which go on continually and which at present center chiefly in the Far East.

REFERENCE NOTES

CHAPTER I

1. Karl Marx, *Capital*, Vol. III, Charles H. Kerr, p. 953.
2. Karl Marx, *Value, Price and Profit*, p. 84.
3. Karl Marx, *Capital*, Vol. I, International Publishers, p. 715.
4. *See* Charlotte Todes, *The Injunction Menace*, International Pamphlets, No. 22.
5. *The Yellow-Dog Contract*, Elliot E. Cohen, International Pamphlets, No. 21.
6. Karl Marx, *The Civil War in France*, Postgate's edition, p. 29.
7. Karl Marx, *Wage-Labor and Capital*, International Publishers, p. 48.
8. *Capital*, Vol. I, p. 320.
9. Charles and Mary Beard, *Rise of American Civilization*, p. 132.
10. Kathleen Simon, *Slavery*, p. 128.
11. *Capital*, Vol. III, p. 158.
12. New York *Times*, October 5, 1931.
13. See 1929 Report of Institute for Government Research; *Massacre*, by Robert Gessner; article in *Survey Graphic*, January, 1929; *Good Housekeeping*, February and March, 1929.

CHAPTER II

1. Austin H. MacCormick, "Education in the Prisons of Tomorrow," chapter in *Prisons of Tomorrow, Annals of the American Academy for Political and Social Science*, September, 1931, p. 73.
2. New York *Times*, July 13, 1932.
3. New York *World-Telegram*, July 10, 1931.
4. *See* Vern Smith, *The Frame-Up System*, International Pamphlets, No. 8.

CHAPTER III

1. New York *Times*, March 27, 1932.
2. New York *World-Telegram*, August 29, 1931.
3. Based largely on *Handbook of American Prisons and Reformatories*, 1929.
4. Howard B. Gill, "Convict Labor," chapter in *Prisons of Tomorrow*, pp. 83-101.
5. New York *Times*, August 22, 1892.

CHAPTER IV

1. New York *Times*, October 24, 1931.
2. *Report of National Commission on Law Observance and Enforcement* (Wickersham Commission), Vol. IX, pp. 109-110.

3. United States Children's Bureau, *Bulletin*, No. 182, 1928, p. 34.
4. New York *Times*, November 18, 1931.
5. J. S. Allen, *The American Negro*, International Pamphlets, No. 18, p. 3.
6. *Prisons of Tomorrow*, p. 25.
7. *Churchman*, January 31, February 7, 1931.
8. Leon Whipple, *Story of Civil Liberties in the United States*, pp. 290-291.
9. *Ibid.*, p. 236.
10. Anna Rochester, *Labor and Coal*, p. 179.
11. Knoxville *News-Sentinel*, February, 1931.

CHAPTER V

1. From a typewritten manuscript in hands of Esther Lowell, author of *Labor in the South*, International Publishers. Included in material gathered by North Carolina State Board of Charities.

CHAPTER VI

1. Herbert J. Seligman, *The Negro Faces America*, p. 222.
2. Statement by a former United States attorney in Arkansas, quoted by Seligman, *op. cit.*, pp. 247-248.
3. Carter G. Woodson, *The Rural Negro*, p. 49.
4. *Ibid.*, pp. 72-73.
5. *Ibid.*, p. 75.
6. New York *World*, November 24, 1929.
7. *Federated Press*, December 7, 1929.
8. United States Department of Labor, Division of Negro Economics, *Negro Migrations in 1916-17*, p. 104.
9. *International Labor News Service*, August 9, 1930.
10. Memphis *Press-Scimitar*, April 18, 1931. See also *American Labor Banner*, March 7, 1931.
11. Thomas J. Michie, editor, *Georgia Code*, 1926, Penal Code, Section 125 (P 122), p. 1926.
12. *Ibid.*, Section 715, p. 2037.
13. *Ibid.*, Section 716, p. 2037.
14. 219 U.S. 219 Bailey *v.* State of Alabama.
15. Alabama laws as amended in 1907, cited in 219 U.S. 219 Bailey *v.* State of Alabama.
16. Florida, *Cumulative Statutes, 1925*, Section 5161.
17. New York *World*, November 24, 1929.
18. Jerome Dowd, *The Negro in American Life*, chapter on Peonage, pp. 133-134.

CHAPTER VII

1. Woodson, *op. cit.*, p. 78.
2. *Ibid.*, p. 78.
3. Immigration Commission, *Peonage*, pp. 439-449 of Senate Document No. 747, Vol. II, 61st Congress, 3rd Session.
4. *The Crisis*, July, 1920, p. 139.
5. Monroe Work, *Negro Yearbook*, 1931-32, pp. 139-141.

6. New York *Times,* February 2, 1927.
7. Work, *op. cit.,* pp. 139-141.
8. *The Crisis,* January, February and March, 1928; also Woodson, *op. cit.,* pp. 86-88.
9. *Hearings on the Restriction of Western Hemisphere Immigration,* before Committee on Immigration, U. S. Senate, 70th Congress, First Session, p. 42.
10. *The Crisis,* January, February, March, 1928.
11. New York *Times,* February 4, 1931.
12. *Ibid.*
13. New Orleans *Times-Picayune,* February 17, 1931.
14. Woodson, *op. cit.,* p. 88.
15. New York *World,* November 24, 1929.
16. Knoxville (Tennessee) *News-Sentinel,* March 27, 1930.
17. New York *Sun,* December 2, 1931; also *Associated Press* report, December 4, 1931.
18. *See* Moore *et al v.* Dempsey, 261 U.S. 86.
19. Seligman, *op. cit.,* p. 234.
20. Charlotte Todes, *Labor and Lumber,* pp. 174-178.
21. Seligman, *op. cit.,* p. 317.
22. Allen, *op. cit.,* p. 13.
23. Knoxville (Tenn.) *News-Sentinel,* February 22, 1931.
24. Paul S. Taylor, *Mexican Labor in the United States: Imperial Valley,* University of California Press, 1928, pp. 45-52.
25. Labor Research Association, *Labor Fact Book,* p. 157.

CHAPTER VIII

1. Walter H. Liggett, *The Rise of Herbert Hoover,* pp. 137-138.
2. *Ibid., p.* 211.
3. John Hamill, *The Strange Career of Mr. Hoover,* p. 160 *ff.*
4. For a discussion of American imperialism in these countries see *Labor Fact Book,* pp. 35-42.
5. Jessie Lloyd, *Federated Press,* November 19, 1930.
6. *The Nation,* May 23, 1928.
7. *Current History,* March, 1922.
8. Dana G. Munro, *The Five Republics of Central America,* p. 60 *ff.*
9. Quoted by Carleton Beals in *Current History,* August, 1930.
10. *Report of International Commission of Inquiry into the Existence of Slavery and Forced Labor in the Republic of Liberia, 1930.* The report was also summarized in *Monthly Labor Review,* May, 1931, pp. 58-62.
11. R. L. Buell, *The Native Problem in Africa,* p. 834.
12. *Current History,* April, 1929.
13. Leo L. Partlow, *Asia,* January, 1931.
14. Washington *Times,* August 11, 1921.
15. United States Bureau of Labor Statistics, *Bulletin* No. 534, *Labor Conditions in Hawaii,* p. 15.
16. The American Chamber of Commerce *Journal,* June, 1930.
17. Moorfield Storey and Marcial P. Lichauco, *The Philippines and the United States,* p. 25 *ff.*
18. R. L. Buell, New York *Times,* December 15, 1929.
19. *Federated Press,* September 1, 1926.

CHAPTER IX

1. From a speech delivered by Joseph Stalin, February 4, 1931, in Moscow at the First All-Russian Conference of Workers in Socialist Industrialization.
2. *Statement of John L. Spivak, Presented to the Congressional Committee Investigating Communist Propaganda, July 24, 1930,* American Civil Liberties Union (mimeographed).
3. *New Republic,* February 25, 1931, quoting *Manchester Guardian.*
4. *Forced Labor in Russia?* published by *British-Russian Gazette and Trade Outlook,* London, pp. 37-42.
5. See *Russian Timber,* report of the Delegation Appointed by the Russian Timber Committee of the Timber Trade Federation of the United Kingdom.
6. *United States Daily,* October 26, 1931.
7. New York *Times,* April 10, 1932.
8. New York *Times,* June 6, 1932.
9. Joseph Freeman, *The Soviet Worker,* International Publishers, p. 254.
10. New York *World-Telegram,* July 30, 1931.
11. Roger N. Baldwin, *Liberty Under the Soviets,* p. 248.
12. New York *Times,* January 19, 1931.
13. George M. Price, *Labor Protection in the Soviet Union,* p. 55; see also *Soviet Trade Unions* by Robert W. Dunn.
14. Joseph Freeman, *op. cit.,* pp. 188-189.
15. *Ibid.,* pp. 188-189.
16. New York *Times,* July 5, 1931.

INDEX

187

THE END